THE CONFIDENT WRITER
WRITER
A Norton Workbook

AMY RICHARDS

WAYNE STATE UNIVERSITY

Second Edition

W · W · NORTON & COMPANY · NEW YORK · LONDON

THE CONFIDENT WRITER
WRITER
A Norton Workbook

Second Edition

Printed in the United States of America.

ISBN 0-393-95620-2

W. W. Norton & Company, Inc., 500 Fifth Avenue, New York, N.Y. 10110
W. W. Norton & Company Ltd., 37 Great Russell Street, London WC1B 3NU

2 3 4 5 6 7 8 9 0

CONTENTS

* Corresponding sections of *The Confident Writer: A Norton Handbook* are indicated in parentheses.

3. BASIC SENTENCE GRAMMAR: WORD CLASSES   51

4. BASIC SENTENCE GRAMMAR: PHRASES, CLAUSES, AND SENTENCES

5. PROBLEMS WITH VERBS

6. PROBLEMS WITH NOUNS AND PRONOUNS

7. PROBLEMS WITH AGREEMENT

8. PROBLEMS WITH MODIFIERS

13. PUNCTUATING SENTENCES

14. PUNCTUATION OF WORDS

REVIEWING THE WRITING PROCESS

INDEX

PREFACE

The Confident Writer: A Norton Workbook teaches rhetoric, paragraph and sentence structure, effective word choice, grammar, and mechanics through explanation, example, exercise, and writing. In its plan it addresses most of the subjects covered in *The Confident Writer: A Norton Handbook*. It extends the usefulness of the handbook by giving further practice, often through a new or simplified approach, in the understanding of the subjects.

There are five parts to each workbook chapter: summary explanations of the concepts treated in the chapter; examples of these concepts; outlines of the learning objectives for the exercises; exercises; and writing assignments. The summaries and examples review the explanations in the corresponding chapters of the handbook and become a reference source when the workbook is used without the handbook. The list of exercise objectives introduces the reasons for doing the exercises. The exercises themselves give experience in both the recognition of the subject and in its use. Finally, the writing assignments give an opportunity for practicing new understandings and skills in a paragraph or an essay.

You may choose to assign the workbook to the whole class, using it for class discussions and activities throughout the semester. If you do this, you could

- focus on rhetoric in class, assigning chapters 1 and 2 (rhetoric), 9 (Crafting Sentences), 10 (Revising Sentences), 11 (Choosing Effective Words). Chapters on grammar and mechanics could be assigned as a review outside of class;
- focus on paragraphing, sentence structure, grammar, and mechanics, using chapter 2 (Paragraphs and the Writing Process), 3 and 4 (Basic Sentence Grammar), 5, 6, 8 (problems with verbs, nouns and pronouns, and modifiers), 7 (Problems with Agreement), 10 (Revising Sentences), and 12–14 (spelling and punctuation);
- assign only those chapters that are relevant to the needs of your particular class or to your prescribed course syllabus.

Alternatively, you might make the workbook optional, assigning it only to students who need work in special areas.

Since students gain greater insight if they work exercises together, you can encourage group work by
- making a part of a chapter the focus of a class discussion in which answers to exercises are produced by the class;
- dividing a class into groups in which exercises are discussed and worked together;

- assigning to a group the task of explaining a subject to the class, using the exercises for illustrations;
- allowing students who share a common problem to work exercises for that problem in a laboratory or conference;
- promoting an after-class workshop in which students help each other review grammar, punctuation, and sentence structure.

Acknowledgments I would like to thank the many people who helped me with this book: the scores of students whose essays provided the paragraphs and sentences that make up the bulk of the examples and exercises in the workbook; other students who tried out exercises; teachers, Carol Domblewski, Claire Crabtree, and Patricia Hernlund, who contributed in special ways to the preparation of the workbook; its editor, Barry Wade, whose skill and insight shaped the book; Barry's assistants, Victoria Thys and Heather Warren, who cheerfully arranged details; its expert copy editors, Marian Johnson and Jeremy Townsend; and, of course, Connie Gefvert, who guided and supported my efforts.

INTRODUCTION

Writing confidence grows when your readers let you know that they have understood your writing easily and quickly. Confidence increases even more when you learn how you have achieved this readability; if you know what techniques you have used well, you can employ them again to assure future successes. Helping you recognize effective writing techniques is one of the important roles of this workbook.

The Confident Writer: A Norton Workbook gives comprehensive coverage of most of the subjects treated in the *The Confident Writer: A Norton Handbook*. If you are having trouble understanding a particular point in the handbook, you should turn to the workbook for a summary explanation and examples of most topics in addition to exercises and perhaps essay assignments.

The workbook identifies successful rhetorical, paragraph, and sentence structures, and effective word choices, grammar, and mechanics. In addition to identifying these features of writing, the workbook gives you practice in using them effectively. It provides exercises and essay assignments that help you practice using rhetorical skills; building essays, paragraphs, and sentences; and choosing appropriate words, grammatical forms and mechanics.

Each exercise begins with directions that are accompanied by examples of how to follow them. The exercises are often paired, the first helping you recognize the concept being studied, the second asking you to use it in an appropriate form. The exercises have not been constructed so as to trick you, but only to give you practice in recognizing and using forms. Since the examples and the exercise materials have been taken from the writing of college students and have been tried out by college students, you should find them easy to read and relate to. Try to do the exercises not automatically but thoughtfully, reviewing the explanations, examining the examples, and fulfilling the directions with care.

There are many ways in which your instructor may use the workbook: your whole class may work exercises which will be used for class discussions and activities; you may join with other students in workshop sessions where you will help each other master certain concepts; you may be assigned only those sections that are relevant to the course syllabus; or you may be asked to use the workbook on your own to review information.

While using the workbook remember that the exercises are not ends in themselves but steps toward your becoming a more confident writer. Mastering a concept such as when to use "who" or "whom" or how to structure a particular kind of paragraph or sentence will bring a sense of accomplishment, but the real victory comes when you apply what you have learned to your own writing.

1

THE WRITING PROCESS

Do you look around the room at your classmates as they concentrate on an in-class writing project or watch them as they happily hand in a neatly typed term paper and feel that you must be the only one among them who experiences writing as a struggle? The truth of the matter is that most students—and most professional writers too—find writing a complex process and share with you a sense of its difficulties. Although the writing process differs for different writers, most go through a similar series of activities.

- They start out by deciding to explore an experience, develop the answer to a question, interpret an event, convey information, or argue a position in writing.
- Next, they unearth ideas and facts about this subject;
- Assess the purpose and audience of the project;
- Shape a thesis suitable to the purpose;
- Select the ideas for supporting the thesis and the methods for developing and arranging them;
- Allow the subconscious to incubate while it discovers new ideas and new relationships among ideas;
- Draft, redraft and ultimately edit.

While this outline may make the writing process seem complex, take comfort in knowing that you have already mastered many of these activities and regularly engage in them unconsciously. More confidence will come to you when you recognize these activities as they occur and engage in them deliberately, thus producing more thoughtful writing. As you engage in the writing exercises at the end of each chapter in this book, return to this list and check off the steps you recognize yourself performing.

Confidence will come as well with your secure knowledge of paragraph and sentence structure—with your understanding of their coherence and the options for their forms. It will come more easily, furthermore, when you feel assured of grammatical patterns and their relationships and the rationale and rules for punctuation and mechanics. At the end of the workbook you will have the chance to write an essay describing your personal writing process and your mastery of the internal structures of paragraphs and sentences and their punctuation.

Making Choices   (3a–b)*

After you have found your subject and gathered ideas about it, the ideas and information you have discovered can be examined in order to develop a *thesis*. While you develop your thesis, you should consider what the *purpose* of your project will be, its *audience*, and what *medium* you will use.

Finding a Thesis

The *thesis* is an assertion that says something about your subject. It will become your statement of the central idea of your essay. In order to find your thesis, review your body of ideas to be certain what you want your final subject to be. Next, make an assertion about this subject, and you will have found a thesis.

> SUBJECT: Our traditional Fourth of July picnic
> ASSERTION: unifies our extended family.
> THESIS: Our traditional Fourth of July picnic unifies our extended family.

A thesis will be most effective if it is *specific, unified,* and its *scope* and *point of view* are *limited* and *clear*. One student made the following series of revisions in order to arrive at an effective thesis.

> FIRST VERSION: An increase in crime makes problems.

(Subject and assertion are too broad in scope; viewpoint is unclear.)

> SECOND VERSION: An increase in car thefts makes problems.

(Subject is more specific and its scope has narrowed; viewpoint of assertion remains vague.)

> THIRD VERSION: An increase in car thefts makes problems and so does an increase in home fires.

(An idea unrelated to "Crime" destroys the unity of the thesis.)

> FINAL VERSION: *An increase in car thefts results in higher insurance premiums.*

(Both subject and assertion are narrow in scope and more specific. Irrelevant idea has been removed to restore unity.)

Purpose, Medium, and Audience

Once you form your thesis, you must consider other factors that will affect your writing. Three of these factors are *purpose, medium,* and *audience.*

---

* Corresponding sections of *The Confident Writer: A Norton Handbook* are indicated in parentheses.

- *Purpose:* People write for a variety of reasons: to inform someone; to persuade someone; to express themselves or clarify for themselves how they feel; to entertain or please others. Any one or a combination of these may be the *purpose* for writing.
- *Medium:* The *medium* is the form in which the information, expression, or plea is conveyed. Forms of written communication vary from notes and letters to memos, essays, and exam answers.
- *Audience:* The person or group to whom writing is addressed is the *audience.* The audience may be a friend, a fellow worker, an institution, the general public, or yourself.

The *purpose* for which you write a message will often dictate a particular *audience,* and both the purpose and the audience will influence the choice of *medium.* All three variables, therefore, become related factors in composing a piece of writing. For example, the *purpose* of the following *medium* (memo) is to give the *audience* (staff) information (scheduling for the summer months).

This is to inform you officially that the College will operate during the summer months on the basis of a conventional five-day work week. To the extent practicable, classes will be offered Mondays through Thursdays.

Developing the Thesis   (4a–i)

The same body of ideas that produced your thesis also provides many of the ideas that will help develop it (other relevant ideas will occur while you write). Your next step in writing will be to review the ideas you have accumulated and select those which support the thesis. You might even develop a rough plan for your paper as you work, noting where some of the specific ideas belong.

The overall method of developing your essay will follow from the method implied in your thesis. The subsections of your essay may develop by the same or other supporting methods. You will not force a method upon your ideas, but your ideas will relate to each other in ways that suit them to a certain method. When you learn to recognize the methods, you consciously and, thus, more clearly use them in developing your essay. For example, this thesis implies a development by *cause and effect:*

The atmosphere of an intensive care unit makes it difficult for patients to sleep.

As the writer developed the cause and effect relationship between the sounds and sights in the intensive care unit and the patients' inability to sleep, she employed in supporting sections of the essay other methods: *narration, description, process analysis, definition, comparison, contrast, analogy, division analysis, example,* in addition to *cause and effect.*

- *Narration* tells a story. The writer begins her essay by narrating the events that led to her attempt to find sleep in an intensive care unit:

I knew where I was! EMS had picked me out of my totaled truck and rushed me to the emergency room of City Hospital. Now that my body had been repaired in surgery, I was being monitored in the intensive care unit of the hospital. I not only knew where I was, but I also knew that I wanted very much to sleep. The healing balm of sleep, however, operates with difficulty among the alien sights and sounds of an intensive care unit.

- *Description* uses words to show us something as clearly as if we could see, hear, smell, or feel it. In the following paragraph another writer describes a leg brace that she used as a child:

I was glad in one respect that I hadn't given it away, for it was in horrible shape. The leather straps were frayed and tattered, the toe of the brace scuffed up, the padded hip-part falling to pieces with its stuffing loose, and I could still see a golden glint to the metal where the bottom had been soldered over and over again. Like it or not, it had served me long and well.

- *Process analysis* shows the reader how to do something or how something is done. This writer describes how he begins to write an essay:

When I start to write, my mind works in a way that forces me to line up similar things. First, I place all the sharpened pencils on one side of my desk and all the dull ones on the other side. Next, I line my ideas up in the same way. The sharpest ones I put down on paper; the dullest I set aside. Then, I begin to sort out the good ideas, arranging like ideas together.

- *Definition* explains what something is by putting it in a large class and then telling what makes it different from other members of its class. The next writer places women comics in a *class* with entertainers and explains how their humor is *different* from the humor of male entertainers:

Female comedians are the kind of entertainers who put themselves down without offending other people. Male comedians can joke about abortion, racial issues, drugs, and other tragedies, but female humorists cannot. Entertainers like Carol Burnett, Lily Tomlin, Joan Rivers, and Phyllis Diller make fun of ugliness, shrillness, meanness, or vagueness in their own behavior.

- *Comparison* shows similarities between things with a common base. The base for the following comparison exists in the purposes people have for using humor:

People tend to use humor for similar purposes. Some initiate a business meeting with a little joking, and others do the same in a social situation. Many people, when encountering embarrassment in a social or a business event, tend to laugh things off as a form of damage control.

- *Contrast* shows the differences between things with a common base. The common base for the following contrast is work areas and work activities. The writer contrasts both the two work areas in the law offices where she works and the different activities of the workers in each:

The cluttered 15′ × 10′ room is a cornerspace for litigation production and storage, a hole-in-the-wall office that is piled with boxes and shelves of catalogued correspondence reserved for clerky purposes. I am one of four women packed away in this little room, unacknowledged by the fifty or so attorneys at the prestigious law firm. On the other hand, those fifty attorneys greet their clients in spacious offices impressive for their wide sweep from handsome bookshelves to windows to uncluttered desks. They see them again in awesome court rooms, using for their defense materials anonymously delivered from our crowded little room where we are sentenced to do tedious and bothersome work.

- *Analogy* compares something unfamiliar to something familiar in order to explain something about the unfamiliar. This writer compares the act of starting to write to a physical act of daring:

    The act of writing, for my purposes, is like throwing an inflatable raft into whitewater rapids with a rope attached from it to my waist, or, possibly, like the step forward that commits me to the "down" escalator. The initial plunge, whether into the rapids, onto the escalator, or putting pen to paper, is the most difficult part of the process.

- Analysis by *division* breaks something into its component parts in order to explain it. The writer divides his favorite way of spending the Fourth of July into three different categories:

    I have three favorite kinds of Fourth of July, one involving a family picnic, another, a swimming date, and a third, puttering around at home. The picnic is the most fun when the sun is shining and everyone is home from college. The second appeals to me when I am going steady and the weather is hot. The third is best when I am tired, no one else is around, and I have lots of work to do—or if it's raining. The first is a good old-fashioned American Fourth, and I love it; the second, with luck, can be combined with the first but makes a good substitute if the plans for a family picnic fall through; the third is a chance-to-catch-up holiday, very relaxing and with practical merit.

- *Examples* give you a chance to illustrate something general by something very specific or concrete. In this paragraph, examples support the idea that a weekend canoeing trip was fun:

    One of the highlights of the weekend was the canoeing trip. Kate and I ended up with the two cutest guys there, one girl and one guy to a canoe. The four of us did the craziest things. For example, we raced canoes, and Kate lost her sunglasses to an overhanging tree branch; we climbed every third sand dune, exhausting ourselves because there were twenty-seven dunes. We never saw the guys after the camping trip, but we certainly had great fun.

- *Cause-effect analysis* shows the causes of certain events and their results or effects. This writer describes the effect of a childhood crime on his parents' behavior and the effect that the spanking had on him:

    When I got home, my mother was furious. Sandy's mother had called and told her about my stealing spree. I was sent up to my room; my ill-gotten toys were taken from me; and my mother would yell up the stairs every few minutes, "Wait 'til your father gets home." When my father got home, it was like World War II, but instead of bombs exploding, it was the sound of a leather belt against the seat of my jeans. That is how I learned not to take what wasn't mine.

Planning and Arranging   (6a–b)

The way you arrange the ideas which support your thesis will guide readers more clearly towards an understanding of your intentions. A successful arrangement gives emphasis to certain ideas and provides a beginning and ending to the writing. When you recognize and consciously use different arrangements, you gain a greater control over the ordering of ideas in thinking and writing. You also develop an understanding of the choices available in planning essays and other writing.

Ordering Your Writing

Certain principles of order will follow from using certain methods such as *description* or *process*, but each method has more than one possible arrangement of ideas. In an essay or paragraph, you may follow:

• *spatial order* if the subject involves a physical placement of objects;
• *chronological order* if the subject involves a time sequence;
• *order of specificity* if a general statement is followed by details, or if specifics lead up to a general statement;
• *alternating order* if two things are compared and contrasted or an analogy is developed;
• *climactic order* if a dramatic emphasis is desired toward the end;
• *order of familiarity* if a familiar idea introduces the reader to a less familiar idea.

For example, this paragraph in the *descriptive* method follows a *spatial* order:

> For a story I might write someday, I have a little picture that I have saved up in my mind. I was in a subway train stopped at a station. I was looking out of the window at a couple seated on a concrete bench. They were sitting very close together. She had yellow hair that was disagreeably matted. He looked unwashed or perhaps the subway gloom made him look that way. He was putting a ring on her finger as the train left.

This paragraph in the *example* method follows a *chronological* order (The chronology in this paragraph moves from recent to distant time; the reverse is also possible):

> To call *anorexia nervosa* a new disease is not really correct in the literal sense. The illness was described a little over one hundred years ago in England and France and was named by Sir William Gull, a British physician. There are references to still earlier observations. Richard Morton in 1869 reported a case of nervous consumption which seems to be the same illness. In the eighteenth century, as well, cases which seem very like the modern *anorexia nervosa* were described.

Beginnings and Endings

Titles and opening paragraphs satisfy the readers' sense of order by letting them know that something is beginning; ending paragraphs fulfill their need for termination and closure.

Titles become the first introduction to an essay or a report. They are generally made up of a phrase, a word, a short clause, or two clauses separated by a colon. Titles engage the reader's attention, focus on the subject matter, and sometimes cause the reader to ponder while reading the essay.

TITLE	THESIS
Who Lost Cuba?	There are three reasons for the United States having lost control over Cuba.
Night Owl TV: Sex in the Old Movies	Sexual episodes in old movies on late night television should be X-rated.
Overachievers: The Super Mom	Mothers who work too hard at mothering are like workaholics.

Beginning paragraphs give your readers a general introduction to your subject and to the assertion that you make about it. Very often, then, you will include a statement of your thesis in your opening paragraph, making the limits and direction of the essay clear from the beginning. The method of your beginning paragraph may be the same as the dominant method of your paper, but it doesn't have to be. You may decide to *define* your subject before you develop it, or you may want to engage your readers' interest first with an *analogy, narration,* or *description.*

This beginning paragraph describes the setting and characters important to an understanding of the essay it introduces. The paragraph ends with the thesis statement:

> Every Christmas the whole family tries to get together; yet there is always one of us that either has to work or has no money to come home on. This year we finally did it: Billy came home from California; Laurie, from Connecticut; and Jennie from Texas. On Christmas Day, two uncles, two aunts, and their combined families of five children joined us. We had quite a house full, most definitely the largest gathering ever. Dinner was served buffet style, and somehow we all managed to squeeze into the living room, sitting on the floor or wherever we could to balance our plates. *After dinner we spent a long time reminiscing about past Christmases: the funny ones, the tragic ones, and the "political" one, which, this Christmas, became one of the funny ones.*

Often in a short essay a sentence at the end of the last paragraph will function as your ending. In long essays and reports, however, you will need an *ending paragraph.* This paragraph may contain a review of the contents of a lengthy essay, the concluding statement of an argument, the answer to a question asked in the beginning paragraph, a question resulting from the development of the thesis, or an explicit statement of a thesis that has remained implicit throughout. The *arrangement of ideas* in ending paragraphs is often the *climactic* order or the order of *specificity.*

This ending paragraph reviews the points covered in an essay on modern scientists' attitudes toward acupuncture. The order of ideas is climactic:

> It seems, then, that acupuncture, the healing art which originated in Oriental medicine, has become much more than a mysterious needle treatment. Various scientists in biophysics, physiology, neuropsychiatry, and internal and physical medicine have begun to explore its possibilities. The modern practitioners of medicine may shortly find themselves practicing a modern version of the ancient art of acupuncture.

This ending paragraph answers the question asked in a beginning paragraph. The order of ideas is climactic:

> Finally, my answer to the question "Why do I write?" is not that it is an art or a way of life as it is for E. B. White, James Baldwin, or Joan Didion. Writing is for me simply a mode of communicating how I feel about something, a way of getting my important thoughts to someone else.

Exercise Objectives

Developing an effective thesis; distinguishing and using different media, audiences, and purposes; recognizing and practicing the methods of development; recognizing and using the arrangements of ideas; writing titles; analyzing beginnings and endings; recognizing levels of abstraction; writing an outline.

1 THE WRITING PROCESS _____

Name _____ *Date* _____

EXERCISE 1   Shaping a Thesis

The following theses are too broad in scope or point of view, are lacking in
unity, or are not specific enough. On the lines below restate each thesis to make
it more effective.

EXAMPLE
Child abuse is rampant.

The abuse of children by their parents occurs
in all social classes.

_____

1. Students should write application forms early.

_____
_____
_____
_____

2. Exercise brings good health.

_____
_____
_____
_____

3. Planet earth may soon be choked by industrial wastes and, in addition, it
   will be overpopulated.

_____
_____
_____
_____

4. Television is interesting.

_____
_____
_____
_____

5. Rock music is bad for the health, and it has Satanic powers.

_____

_____

_____

6. Animals bring happiness.

_____

_____

_____

7. Teachers deserve a raise in pay.

_____

_____

_____

8. Computers help students to get higher grades.

_____

_____

_____

9. Some cancer patients receive therapy.

_____

_____

_____

10. Ty Cobb was a great figure and so was Joe Louis.

_____

_____

_____

1 THE WRITING PROCESS _____

Name _____ *Date* _____

EXERCISE 2   Rewriting for Different Audiences and Purposes

1. Carefully read the following paragraphs and describe the purpose, medium, and audience of the writing.

> The Megasewee River will crest tonight at record levels. At 3 a.m. this morning it overflowed its banks and swept through the town of Sewee. Waters continue to run past houses now flooded up to the second floor. Mobile homes in Johnson's Park are inundated.
>
> No flooding of such severity has been seen in this area before. The damage already is estimated in the millions.
>
> CB radios and station MBC FM are being used to communicate emergency information. Inhabitants of the homes have been ferried by police and others to Motts Hill High School and housed in the gym. The Red Cross is flying in food and medical supplies, and people from the next county are promising clothing and bedding.
>
> So far no human lives have been lost, but a number of livestock and pets have been swept away. Mr. George McWilliams of 12 River Street, interviewed at the High School, said, "I'm thankful my wife and son are safe, but I am afraid the water has ruined our home and everything we worked to put in it."

PURPOSE: _____

_____

MEDIUM: _____

_____

AUDIENCE: _____

_____

2. From the body of information given in the paragraphs above, select the materials useful for any two of the combinations of purpose, medium, and audience listed below, and compose in the medium indicated. Enter each piece of writing on a separate sheet of paper.
   a. A letter from a victim of the flood asking for help from a family member living elsewhere.
   b. A communication from the police chief to her officers alerting them to problems associated with the flood.
   c. A report of the flood for the historical archives of the town.
   d. An entry into a flood victim's diary in which he expresses his feelings about the flood.

EXERCISE 3   Writing an Essay Describing Thesis, Purpose, Medium, and Audience

In the course of a day's activities pick up any flyers or brochures that you come across. Choose one as the subject of an in-class essay. *Your* purpose in this essay should be to state the thesis and to describe the purpose, medium, and audience of the item chosen. *Reminder:* many considerations play a part in the choice of medium, such as easy and fast reading, physical availability, and cost. Write your essay on separate sheets of paper and clip the brochure or flyer to it for use in group or class discussion.

1 THE WRITING PROCESS

Name _____ Date _____

EXERCISE 4 Recognizing Overall Methods of Development

First, examine each of the following theses for the relationship of ideas existing within it. Next, identify the dominant method suggested by this relationship and write it on the line below. (After finishing, fill in "method" in exercise 1.)

EXAMPLE

THESIS: You can change the oil in your car yourself.

METHOD: _*process*_ _____

1. I am at times a basketball player and at times a coach; the two roles make different demands on me, but they are both fun.

   METHOD: _____

2. Living with Marianne is like playing golf in a thunderstorm.

   METHOD: _____

3. Birth order has an effect on a person's success in life.

   METHOD: _____

4. There are two kinds of courses I will never take again.

   METHOD: _____

5. Computer writing demands a knowledge both of how to write and how to use a computer.

   METHOD: _____

6. Investigators found the cause of the plane crash to be engine failure.

   METHOD: _____

7. The traveler pictured Tokyo as noisy and colorful.

   METHOD: _____

8. We must first know what terrorism is; then we can deal with it.

   METHOD: _____

9. The difference between novels and short stories lies partly in length.

   METHOD: _____

10. There are three ways of getting to Chicago.

    METHOD: _____

EXERCISE 5 Using Methods of Development

Two theses are given in each of the items below. Each group of theses implies a dominant method of development. Choose one thesis from each item and develop a paragraph using it. Identify the method you use.

EXAMPLE
My cat is beautiful.
I was impressed by the charm (elegance, ugliness) of the family room.

METHOD: *description*

I stepped back two steps and looked at him somewhat searchingly as one might look at a painting. Muffy looked back at me with his big, green, inquisitive, unblinking eyes. Actually he was quite a beautiful creature – he was huge for a house cat and all white with curtains of gray thrown casually about his shoulders and masking his eyes.

1. There are three kinds of architecture in my neighborhood.
   My week is characterized by four different kinds of labor.

   METHOD: _____

   _____

   _____

   _____

   _____

   _____

2. My mom is an overachiever.
   Weird (tired, excited) people crammed the (bus, airport, doctor's) waiting room.

   METHOD: _____

   _____

   _____

   _____

   _____

3. The process of registration is something you should know about ahead of time.

My roommate (sister, child, uncle) has mastered the art of avoiding work (paying back loans, punishment, getting places on time, picking up clothes).

METHOD: _____

_____

_____

_____

_____

4. Both the Q and the Z car are high quality vehicles, but they are intended for entirely different uses.

When I compare my elementary school with my high school experiences, I am amazed that I survived either but for different reasons.

METHOD: _____

_____

_____

_____

_____

5. Some unfortunate misunderstandings have arisen because people don't know what a computer hacker is.

Music is more than a series of sounds.

METHOD: _____

_____

_____

_____

_____

EXERCISE 6 Focusing on Methods in Your Own Writing

You have probably made many scattered comments about college life to yourself and your friends. If you organize and develop some of these observations into essay form, you can offer to your classmates a subject for a discussion that may give the whole class a greater insight into the college experience. You might develop your thesis on one of the following subjects.

The problems of financial dependence (or independence)
What constitutes an easy or difficult class
The difference between college and highschool or college and a job
The kinds of people found on campus
How to get through registration

After you have decided on your subject, developed it into a thesis, and gathered your ideas, identify and note the overall method that your thesis requires. For example for the thesis *The kinds of students found in most classrooms are talkers, watchers, or sleepers* the identified method would be *classification*. Note that the development of separate paragraphs within the essay might be made with other methods such as *comparison, example,* or *analogy.*

Name _____ *Date* _____

EXERCISE 7   Practicing Different Orders of Ideas

Groups of scattered notes are listed below. Rearrange each list as directed, and write the paragraph on the lines below.

1. Dominant method is *process;* arrangement is *spatial.*
NOTES: The most efficient way of managing in this small office is to work in clockwise fashion.
First step is "work-received."
Last step is coffee maker, where you can take fifteen-minute break and then you are back at "work-received."
Before you get to coffee maker, you are in front of waist-high filing cabinets where you file the copies you have just made.
From the work-received area, you move to the typewriter where you type the memo you will next run off.
You sit on a swivel chair.

_____

_____

_____

_____

_____

_____

_____

_____

_____

_____

_____

_____

_____

_____

_____

_____

_____

_____

2. Dominant method is *narrative;* arrangement is *chronological.*

NOTES: My aunt had promised to take me on a Caribbean trip.

The day had finally arrived.

On May 17, my parents drove my aunt and me to the airport.

I kissed my parents good-bye and boarded the 727 that would take us to Florida, where we would embark on the cruise ship.

The airport was busy—excited travelers inquiring about seating, time of departure, boarding gate.

All during those cold winter days, I had seen myself sunbathing on the deck of a ship sailing the Caribbean.

It seemed to me that from November to May had been an eternity.

Within twenty-four hours of those good-byes, we were walking up the gang-plank of the *Princess II.*

_____

_____

_____

_____

_____

_____

_____

_____

3. Dominant method is *contrast;* arrangement is *alternative.*

NOTES: Feeding is another area in which we keep more distance between ourselves and our children than do many other societies.

Many of our babies are bottle-fed.

Some are not held but drink from a bottle propped up beside them in a crib.

In many societies, all babies are breast-fed by the mother or a mother substitute.

We often wean a child from the breast at nine months.

These other societies never wean a child before the age of two; sometimes they don't wean until babies are four years.

_____

_____

_____

_____

_____

_____

_____

4. Dominant method is *definition;* Arrangement is from *familiar* to *unfamiliar.*
NOTES: Even if your experience came through watching television, you have
an idea of what one part of my job is like.

Just one of my tasks is what you have seen at the street-accident site, the
rapid assessment of the condition of injury victims and their transport to
the hospital.

I am not a doctor.

I am a paramedic, a specialist in trauma, working for an emergency medical
business.

How many times have you heard the emergency medical service's siren wail-
ing in the distance?

Was there a time when you saw the van stop and watched figures jump from
it, bend over an injured figure, and then rapidly move it to a stretcher and
into the truck?

My job also involves other life-saving activities performed in the truck on
the way to the hospital and in the emergency room.

_____

_____

_____

_____

_____

_____

_____

_____

_____

_____

_____

_____

_____

_____

_____

_____

_____

_____

_____

_____

5. Dominant method is *example;* arrangement is from *general* to *specific.*
   NOTES: Now you can tell the six-foot, six-inch, 250-pound man who tries to shove you out of line at the pop stand, "Look buster, I was here first."
   You can say to the airline stewardess, "I don't care how nice you are, I am still afraid your big, steel bird will crash with me in it."
   You can snarl at the lab assistant, "I am going to kill those dreadful little mice in the cages if they even look at me."
   It is exhilarating when you are no longer afraid to say the things you want to say.

_____

_____

_____

_____

_____

_____

_____

_____

_____

_____

_____

_____

1 THE WRITING PROCESS _____

Name _____ *Date* _____

EXERCISE 8   Writing Paragraphs Using Specified Orders of Ideas

Write paragraphs as indicated below.

1. Divide your life into three significant periods and identify the importance of each. Use chronological arrangement of ideas.

_____

_____

_____

_____

_____

_____

_____

_____

_____

2. Explain to a ten-year-old child how to play a game he or she is unfamiliar with. Use an example of or an analogy to something familiar to start your paragraph.

_____

_____

_____

_____

_____

_____

_____

_____

_____

_____

3. Compare and contrast two friends, teachers, children, or siblings. Use alternative arrangement of ideas and climax the paragraph with the major differences of your subjects.

_____

_____

_____

_____

_____

_____

_____

_____

4. Construct a paragraph of examples which illustrate a generalization such as "My former friend Joe (Sue, Bill, Mrs. Smith) always says what's on his mind," or "Today was the worst of all possible Mondays." Arrange the generalization and the examples so that the order is from specific to general.

_____

_____

_____

_____

_____

_____

_____

_____

5. Observe the room you are sitting in. Find a word that suits the effect the room has on you (crowded, comfortable, depressing). Describe how the spatial arrangements in the room contribute to the effect. (You may choose another space, such as an airplane cabin, a view from the top floor of a building, a subway, or a prairie.)

_____

_____

_____

_____

_____

_____

_____

Name _____ *Date* _____

EXERCISE 9 Creating Titles

The following paragraphs introduce student essays. Create a title based on the paragraph, and write the title on the line preceding the paragraph. Remember that the first and last words and all other important words in a title are capitalized. Articles and short prepositions are not capitalized. Quotation marks and underlining are only used with titles when they are included within the text.

1. TITLE: _____

_____

Father Jack sauntered down to the bus station, and there he saw the girls, blowing bubble gum and giggling. Aware of his approach, they shifted a little nervously as if to run in unison down High Road at the hint of condemnation in his voice. After all, they were skipping school to watch the band arrive from Atlanta, and he was their parish priest!

2. TITLE: _____

_____

How did I end up with a sterilizer filled, not only with water, but also with hundreds of tiny beads of glass and mercury? After I had finished polishing the chrome door handles with alcohol, I spotted thirty-six neatly arranged thermometers. You are right! I decided to clean them all, and gathering them I carefully placed them in the sterilizer. I closed the lid of the container and turned it on. When I lifted the lid after four minutes at 212 degrees, there were the shattered thermometers. That was only the first incident in my disastrous first week as a rookie nurse.

3. TITLE: _____

_____

I can't help but cringe when *Time* or *Newsweek* announces that lawyers, not criminals, mop up the floors. My problem is that I am going into law, a profession that is now glutted with job-seeking lawyers. Shall I continue with the possibility that I may end up mopping floors, or shall I shift goals now?

4. TITLE: _____

_____

The reaction of Americans to the wedding of Prince Charles and Lady Diana serves as an indicator of some of the basic values of our society. Our interest in the event shows our involvement with marriage and family. In fact, for a while Charles and Diana's preparations, nuptials, and honeymoon became as close as the same events in our own families. The royal wedding also showed that Americans must be traditionalists, many of them watching all features of the ceremony for hours on television.

5. TITLE: _____

Never before had I felt myself driven to recall the experience of knowing Emmy. Recently, though, I've been thinking about her. I've been thinking about the kinds of things she did to me. She smoked cigarettes and made me smoke them too—and drink the brew. Now months after Emmy and I broke up, I've quit the smokes and the brew, and I know I have to write about Emmy and me.

6. TITLE: _____

As a sales person who travels extensively around the metropolitan area, Berke finds having a phone in her car very practical. Like top automobile executives and the city mayor, she now can do business during travel time. In addition, she can follow up leads immediately if she is travelling in the area where the call is made.

7. TITLE: _____

The story of the Green Hills Investment operation has the makings of a prime-time television drama replete with corporate jets, a helicopter, and expensive cars. All of these are owned by E. G. McGlee, who now stands indicted of bilking investors out of $40 million.

1 THE WRITING PROCESS ———————————

Name ————————————————— Date —————————

EXERCISE 10   Examining Beginnings and Endings

Examine the following beginning and ending paragraphs of four essays. a) In the *beginning* paragraph, identify the order of ideas. b) Under the *ending* paragraph, describe what the paragraph does: *reviews the essay contents; makes a final point, concludes an argument, answers a question* asked at the beginning of the essay; *makes an explicit statement* of an implicit theme; or *asks a question* raised by the essay.

1. BEGINNING: I barely have enough money to pay my rent and the rest of the bills. I have spent the beginning of the semester living on peanut butter and jelly sandwiches. I am still borrowing the books for psychology from a friend who is also taking the course. But, my tuition has been paid, paid, in fact, from the day I registered.

ORDER OF IDEAS: ————————————————————

————————————————————————————————

ENDING: Skimping after paying my tuition was hard, but it wasn't demeaning. I am proud that, although I didn't manage my money well, I *did* manage it. Living on the edge of economic disaster sharpened my appreciation of the dollar and the education it pays for.

WHAT THE PARAGRAPH DOES: ———————————————

————————————————————————————————

2. BEGINNING: She is our Great-Great-Aunt Sarah, but we call her G.G. Sarah. Although she has to be old and she bakes delicious cookies, G.G. Sarah is not a sweet, old lady, nor was she a sweet young one.

ORDER OF IDEAS: ————————————————————

————————————————————————————————

ENDING: G.G. Sarah is not a proper model for her nieces, but she is a survivor. In her gutsy way she has survived the Depression of the thirties, husbands, boyfriends, and illnesses, and she maintains her outspoken presence in our family in her ninety-eighth year. Could she be the best kind of model after all?

WHAT THE PARAGRAPH DOES: ———————————————

————————————————————————————————

3. BEGINNING: Threatened with rape, would you scream and fight or try to talk him out of it? Traditionally, women have been advised by experts that the most effective response to an attempt at rape is to try to talk the rapist out of his intentions. The reasoning behind the advice is that a woman's resistance will anger the rapist who will respond with more severe physical harm than he had originally intended. Warning women that screaming and

27

fighting will only antagonize the rapist is actually dangerous advice. Women should be taught how to resist rape.

ORDER OF IDEAS: _____

_____

ENDING: A self-defense class will teach women that they have several options when threatened. Acting passively might be one of them, but there are others, and the factors surrounding the attack will dictate whether the woman runs, screams, fights back, or submits.

WHAT THE PARAGRAPH DOES: _____

_____

4. BEGINNING: I know right away what Joe wants. He has come to pick up the papers for the morning drop. One of the other carriers quit last night, and it is Joe's job to see that the papers are delivered. I hand them to him, and without a word passing between us, he is gone.

ORDER OF IDEAS: _____

_____

ENDING: At the very last, I know what Joe wants; again I hand him papers, this time Marine papers that signal his departure to Lebanon; and he is gone. Strange how we fill roles in our relationships to people we love, roles like helper to doer or facilitator to performer, roles that stay with us to the end.

WHAT THE PARAGRAPH DOES: _____

_____

5. BEGINNING: One of the last things you see when you go under an anesthetic in an operating room is the blurred movement of the nurses. There are two kinds of nurses in the surgical unit, the scrub nurses and circulating nurses; each has special jobs assigned that rarely overlap. The success of your operation depends in part on these nurses doing their specific jobs.

ORDER OF IDEAS: _____

_____

ENDING: Finally, along with their separate duties, the scrub nurse and circulating nurse have duties they must perform together. Both nurses participate in the initial and final count of sponges, needles, and instruments. Both are responsible for maintaining a neat and orderly sterile field and for facilitating the availability of instruments. The most important factor of all is that they share a spirit of mutual cooperation essential to the patient's best interest.

WHAT THE PARAGRAPH DOES: _____

_____

_____

Name ─────────────────────── *Date* ───────────

EXERCISE 11 Evaluating Introductions

Imagine that you have been handed the complete essays which are represented in exercise 10 by their beginnings and endings; you will have time to read only two of them. Which two will you read? Base your decision on the effect that the introductions have on you. Now, discuss in paragraph form the reasons for the paragraphs' effect on you. The reasons can be subjective (you are interested in the subject) and objective (the structure of the paragraph). Write your discussion below.

EXERCISE 12   Arranging Your Writing

Read the essay you were assigned in Exercise 3. Examine the arrangement of ideas overall and in each paragraph, revising for easier reading. Write an interesting introduction which predicts the content of the essay and a conclusion which clearly terminates the discussion. Add a title that announces the contents of the essay.

2

PARAGRAPHS AND THE WRITING PROCESS

This chapter can help your writing at many points—where you are forming subsections to support your thesis, where you are dividing large sections into readable chunks, or where you are questioning the completeness or clarity of a supporting section. These sections on writing paragraphs will also help you if you have singled out the composing of such units as a problem. In addition you will find that understanding paragraph structure and coherence will help you understand essay structure and coherence.

Paragraphs as Extended Sentences (11a)

You can think of a paragraph as an extended sentence because the subject and verb of a sentence with its supporting phrases and clauses can be expanded into a paragraph. The subject and verb of the sentence can form a topic sentence for the paragraph, and the phrases and clauses will become its supporting sentences. The sentence or the paragraph will be unified if it excludes material that does not support the subject and verb or the topic sentence.

SENTENCE: *You can tell who has children on our block by the front lawns,* the childless Pollacks having a beautiful, green, weeded lawn cut carefully in diagonal swaths and the Snyders having a green lawn, cut to be sure, but with groups of dandelion heads, tall, upright, and resistant to the mower, sprouting up around the bigwheels, a baseball bat, and four flat stones marking bases.

PARAGRAPH: *You can tell who has children on our block by the front lawns.* The childless Pollacks, for example, have a beautiful, green, weeded lawn cut carefully in diagonal swaths. The Snyders also have a green lawn, cut to be sure, but with groups of dandelion heads, tall and upright, resistant to the mower. These dandelions sprout up around two bigwheels, a baseball bat, and four flat stones marking bases.

Paragraphs as Miniature Essays (11b)

You can view a paragraph as a miniature essay that is self-contained and has relevance, clear order and completeness. The topic sentence acts in the paragraph as a thesis does in an essay.

TOPIC SENCENCE: *Dictionaries contain much information that is helpful to you as a writer.* There are many kinds of dictionaries, but the one you will use most often as you write your essays is a college dictionary. Your college dictionary has the answers to many of the problems you will find in revising and editing your writing: how to spell a word; what its function is; what it means; how to separate it into syllables; whether a verb is transitive or intransitive; and whether a compound word is hyphenated or not. In this dictionary you can also look up punctuation rules, how to write Roman numerals, and such things as the American equivalents of the metric system.

You can also view paragraphs as following one of the basic structures, the *topic, problem* or *question* becoming the topic sentence.

Topic + Restriction + Illustration (TRI)
Problem + Solution (PS)
Question + Answer (QA)
or a combination of these structures such as: PSI or TQAI

T: My favorite time of day is from 7:00 P.M. to 9:00 P.M.
R: This is my cooling out period which I selfishly and joyfully set aside for me.
I: If I want to lock myself in my room and read a book, I do so, knowing that I'm reading it for my satisfaction, not for Ms. Anderson's speech class. If I want to polish my fingernails, I polish them without having to be bothered by any interruptions. If I feel like singing or dancing, I sing or dance. Whatever I feel like doing between the hours of seven to nine, I do because that is my cooling out time.

Paragraphing as Punctuation   (11c)

You can use paragraphs to signal the logical relationships within your essay and to serve as transition between two parts of an essay. In other kinds of writing, they can be shaped to save space or to make sections easier to read.

Paragraphs as Parts of Essays   (12a)

Your essays and the paragraphs in them are easier to understand if they are *coherent* or hold together. The principles of coherence are:

• *Unity:* Every sentence in a paragraph should relate to the topic sentence; every paragraph in the essay should relate to the thesis.
• *Completeness:* Every paragraph in the essay should be complete; every essay should fully develop the thesis.
• *Structure:* Paragraphs should have an orderly arrangement of ideas that support the topic sentence; essays should have an orderly arrangement of paragraphs supporting the thesis.
• *Relationships:* Each paragraph should show clear relationships among the ideas in it; all paragraphs in an essay should show the relationships among each other that enable them to support the thesis.

Transitional Words and Phrases   (12b)

Transitional words and phrases express certain relationships among ideas.

Narration and process analysis: *after, again, during, every time, first, next, second, the next day, then, while.*

Description: *behind, in back of, inside, on the left side, on top, over, under.*

Comparison: *also, comparable, either . . . or, likewise, nor, similarly.*

Contrast: *but, however, in comparison, in contrast, more, on the other hand, rather, unlike, less.*

Cause and effect: *as a result, because, consequently, hence, therefore, thus.*

Division: *after, before, final, first, next, second, then.*

Example: *as, for example, for instance, like, such as, thus, to illustrate.*

Referential Words and Phrases   (12c)

Pronouns pointing to something referred to earlier and adjectives and nouns substituting for previously stated words help hold writing together.

A marriage ceremony in [Telkaif] is prefaced by ritual. In this [small village in Iraq], the knowledge that a union is being considered comes when the man visits the girl's family asking for her hand

To insure coherence, pronouns should agree with antecedents in number and person. When it is not clear what antecedent a pronoun refers to, an appropriate noun or pronoun should be used in place of the confusing pronoun.

> A chocolate lover goes on chocolate binges. They can't stop eating after opening a box of candy. They may last several days or until they get sick.

would be clearer as:

> A chocolate lover goes on chocolate binges. *He or she* can't stop eating after opening a box of candy. *The binges* may last several days or until the *chocolate lover* gets sick.

Repetition of Words and Word Patterns   (12d)

The repetition of significant words and parallel patterns gives coherence to your writing. In the following analogy, the significant word "control" is repeated at three important points. Parallel "if" clauses are repeated in two separate sentences, holding these two sentences together. In addition, the two sentences are parallel because of the similarity of their structures, the "if" clauses, the dash, the understood "there is," and the end word "disaster."

> The element of *control* is of supreme importance when I write. This *control* is like a fireman's ability to rappel himself by rope down the side of a ten-story

building. If the wind blows, if the rope breaks, if his attention is diverted—disaster. Control in writing, for me, also is a kind of synchronized danger. If the ideas don't mesh, if there are too many conflicting ideas, if my attention is diverted—disaster.

Ellipsis (12e)

The omission of part of a clause or phrase, especially if it is parallel to another, helps achieve coherence in writing.

> The men had planned on playing hockey, but Matthew wouldn't play [hockey], and, as a result, Tom wouldn't [play hockey] either.

Exercise Objectives

Expanding sentences into paragraphs; recognizing unity in paragraphs; structuring paragraphs; using paragraphs as punctuation; recognizing and using transitional words in paragraphs, referential words, effectively repeated words and patterns, and ellipses.

2 PARAGRAPHS

Name _____ *Date* _____

EXERCISE 1   Expanding Sentences into Paragraphs

Revise the following sentences so that they become paragraphs. Write the new paragraph on the lines below using the subject and verb of the sentence as the topic sentence of the paragraph.

1. I am the middle child of seven children which has resulted in my being bullied by the older three and my bullying the three younger, my being cared for by the older and my caring for the younger, and ultimately, in my learning how to stand up for myself and how to assume the responsibility of others.

_____

_____

_____

_____

2. Nurse-midwives, who are registered nurses with two years of extra training in obstetrics, have the special appeal of being able to work within the hospital and still provide the woman with the kind of personal structure that makes her feel like a human being and not an object.

_____

_____

_____

_____

3. T. P., who is one of the most conceited guys ever to graduate from Northern High School, started out as a nice guy able to cope with his popularity without getting a big head even though he was voted the most popular student three years in a row, but when he reached his senior year, his head blew up like a balloon.

_____

_____

_____

_____

EXERCISE 2   Finding Topic Sentences

In the following paragraphs find and underline the topic sentence. Because the topic sentence is not always first, look for the sentence that embodies the main idea of the paragraph.

1. A menu in a computer software program is like a menu in a restaurant, a list of choices. From the first menu in my word processing program, I can choose one of several tasks which include opening a new file, saving a document, and printing a file just by pointing to the task on the menu. On the second menu appear my options for editing which involve cutting copy, copying it, or pasting it into a different place in my text. On the other menus are choices for print fonts, style, and alignments. The menus make my options clear; all I have to do is decide which one I want.

2. The mallard ducks and the Canada geese are gathering in flight groups preparing for their migrations. A few monarch butterflies have begun to gather on the trees in expectation of their flight. The leaves have not yet browned or fallen, but their nuts, mostly acorn and pig nuts, have begun to litter the ground. The signs that autumn is very near are all around us.

3. They never forget my birthday, always making plans for a special meal out. They listen to my endless complaints about Jim or my job. Clearly, Beth and Dick are very good friends, even though they can sometimes be exasperating. They were just that last week when they borrowed my car, used up a tank full of gas, and didn't get it back to me on Monday morning in time for me to drive to work.

2 PARAGRAPHS

Name _____ *Date* _____

EXERCISE 3 Recognizing and Using the Three Basic Structures

The first two paragraphs below are constructed according to one of the basic patterns. Identify each sentence of the pattern and write the basic structure on the line below. The last three items below are sentence groups. Combine each group of sentences to make a paragraph following the structure indicated. You may have to revise sentences to make the paragraph clear.

1. What jobs must a medical technician perform? Many routine procedures are involved in a day's work. One group of tasks has to do with the sterilization of equipment. Another has to do with the tests made on body fluids. The task which affects all others is to maintain absolute accuracy in what is being done.

   _____

2. Human beings are social animals and as such they live together. Living together cannot be done without some attendant problems. For example, in the social colonies called cities some individuals prey on others with the result that a police force must be developed to protect the potential victims and restrain the victimizers.

   _____

3. Rewrite as TQA: Where do they work, and what do they have to do with animals?
   The answer to the second is that they maintain the health of animals in both of these places and operate technical machines for anesthesia, X ray, blood counts, and microscopes in order to conduct experiments and diagnose the illness of animals.
   Animal technicians are professionals who must complete a two-year program at a college and pass a state board exam.
   The answer to the first question is that they are found in veterinary practices and animal laboratories.

   _____

   _____

   _____

   _____

   _____

   _____

   _____

   _____

   _____

   _____

4. Rewrite as PSI: Some of you may have trouble finding a non-contact sport that gives exercise to your whole body.
   In addition, the exercising of the limbs, and the effort put into breathing strengthens that all important organ of your body, the heart.
   If this has been your problem, consider the sport of downhill skiing.
   Hips and knees are exercised as the skier gains skill.
   In this sport legs and hip joints and muscles are used in downhill movements, and arms are used in poling on flat land or going up hill.

   _____

   _____

   _____

   _____

   _____

   _____

   _____

   _____

   _____

   _____

5. Rewrite as QAQPS: If you like to tinker, want to save money and don't mind a little grease, you do.
   Who takes care of your car?
   If you do, then where do you do that greasy work?
   But if you live in an apartment, for example, there is no room in your parking spot to spread out your tools and drain the oil.
   If you have your own garage and driveway, you can work on your car there.
   I have the solution—come to Tom Tinker's Garage where you can rent the tools and the space to work.

   _____

   _____

   _____

   _____

   _____

   _____

   _____

   _____

   _____

   _____

2 PARAGRAPHS

Name _____ *Date* _____

EXERCISE 4   Recognizing Unified Paragraphs

The paragraphs 1a and 2a are successfully self contained; Paragraphs 1b and 2b have flaws in them. After comparing each set of paragraphs, identify the flaws in the b paragraphs in terms of the *relevance, completeness,* and *clear order of the ideas.* Write your comments on the lines below.

1a. My mother, an affluent Bolivian lady, asked me why cooking had become so important to me when she had had a cook and a kitchen maid when I was growing up. What I could not make her understand is that once I became a student in America, I saw differences between this country and Bolivia, with the result that I wanted to try some American ways and develop some independence. In learning how to cook, I have discovered that I can care for myself, that I can entertain others, and that I can experiment with different cuisines just for the fun of it.

1b. My mother, an affluent Bolivian lady, asked me why cooking had become so important to me when she had had a cook and a kitchen maid when I was growing up. We had also a gardener and a chauffeur. In learning how to cook, I have discovered that I can entertain others and experiment with different cuisines just for the fun of it.

_____

_____

_____

2a. One of the advantages that a 35 millimeter camera has over the pocket Instamatic is that the negative of the 35 millimeter is approximately two-thirds larger than that of the pocket camera. Although this difference in negative size may not seem significant, it makes a difference when pictures are enlarged. Because the negative of the 35 millimeter is larger, a clear, sharp image is retained on an enlarged print. If, however, the instamatic negative is enlarged to more than a 5″ by 7″ picture, the print will appear dull and grainy. The ability to produce a sizeable enlargement may not seem important to amateur photographers, but, if at some time they produce an especially beautiful shot that they would like to enlarge, they will be happier if they have used a 35 millimeter camera.

2b. One of the advantages that a 35 millimeter camera has over the pocket Instamatic is that the negative of the 35 millimeter is larger. Although this difference in size may not seem significant, it makes a difference when pictures are enlarged. Although the ability to produce a sizeable enlargement may not seem important to amateur photographers, they will be happier if they use a 35 millimeter camera.

_____

_____

_____

EXERCISE 5   Practice in Paragraphing as Punctuation

The following essay is shaped into one paragraph in order to save space. Revise the essay into the paragraph forms you would use for a college essay. Mark the beginning of each paragraph with a paragraph mark (¶), and underline the topic sentence.

A TIME TO UNDERSTAND

Emotional trauma commonly occurs in accident victims. As a result, along with their physical injuries, persons suffer loss of psychological equilibrium. The members of an emergency medical unit must, then, treat accident victims for psychological as well as physical injury. There are two phases of care given injured persons by the medical teams. During the primary-care phase, major injuries to the body are treated and, also, psychological shock and disorganization. During the secondary phase, the treatment of injuries is continued and the psychological problem of depersonalization becomes a paramount consideration. Psychological shock is the patients' reaction to an injury as they try to comprehend what has happened to them. Symptoms include extreme talkativeness which is somewhat incoherent. They also show an unusual calmness and an unawareness of the injury. Treatment is relatively simple: the emergency medical technicians should converse with the patients, responding to them and answering their questions. Disorganization occurs when the shock of the injury begins to wear off. When realization of what has happened to them begins to grow, patients' anxieties rise. Symptoms may include anger or agitation, mild depression and hyperactivity. Each is regarded as a common defense mechanism which helps patients to reorganize their lives. Once again, treatment relies on communication, the constant repetition of explanations concerning treatment being used and the nature of the injury. Depersonalization is also an important result of the treatment of physical injury. Patients become depersonalized or dehumanized when they find themselves hurt and at the mercy of those who are helping them. Patients express feelings of powerlessness, hopelessness, and alienation. They react with anger toward those around them. The emergency medical technician can help persons through the period of depersonalization by listening sympathetically to what is said and, most importantly, by involving the patients in their own physical care. In all cases where the emergency patients are conscious, it is necessary to remember that their emotions as well as their bodies have been hurt. Each person is not "just another accident victim" but a whole human being who needs understanding.

Name _____ *Date* _____

EXERCISE 6   Recognizing and Using Transitional Words and Phrases

Each of the following items has two parts: first, a paragraph for you to analyze for transitional words; and second, directions for writing a paragraph using designated kinds of transitional words.

1. **a.** Underline the transitional words that express time relationships in the following paragraph.

> Throughout the day, my grandmother has been cooking up a feast. When it gets around dinnertime, we hang around the kitchen watching her mix the biscuits, waiting for them to be done. After dinner, the men go into the living room to watch television, smoke, and talk while the women clear the table. Then they all sit around together and talk. After a while, the children gang up on grandfather for stories. As time goes on, the menfolk drift off to sleep while the women go on talking.

   b. Construct a paragraph using words that express time relationships. For your topic consider *the important events of your first few years of life; how you spent several days of a trip; the sequence of courses in mathematics or a foreign language; a simple recipe; how to start a car; how to put together a puzzle.*

_____

_____

_____

_____

_____

_____

_____

_____

2. **a.** Underline the words or phrases that express causal relationships in the following paragraph.

> Theresa enjoys living on other people's money. When it comes down to paying bills, she always claims she is broke, and, as a result, my parents loan her money to pay off her debts. In addition, Theresa gives away half of my belongings, and she once sold my good shoes to her girlfriend. Because I asked her about the shoes, she got angry, saying that she didn't feel she was wrong, and, therefore, would not apologize. As a result of her attitude, I lock my shoes in a drawer and my clothes in a closet.

b. Construct a paragraph using words that express causal relationships. For your topic consider *why you broke up with a friend or lover; why you received your first major punishment as a child; why your garden failed; or why an election was lost.*

_____

_____

_____

_____

_____

_____

_____

_____

3. a. Underline the words and phrases expressing spatial relationships in the following paragraph.

Now inside her room, Josie stands in front of the window and peers at the tiny spots in the distance. Outside on the porch, Tim also stares, attempting to make out how many horses are in the group. Over by the fence, Pa can see the five men and horses. Down by the beech grove, the five men turn toward the house.

b. Construct a paragraph using words that express spatial relationships. For your topic consider *the arrangement of furniture in a room in your house, the location of features in the instrument panel of a car or snowmobile, or the location of the room where your English class is held.*

_____

_____

_____

_____

_____

_____

_____

_____

_____

4. a. Underline the words and phrases expressing comparison and contrast in the following paragraph.

My heart used to beat like this on Christmas morning when I first woke up. Betty and I were about to make our first jet flight to London. It wasn't until we were on board the plane, however, that I realized that, although Betty's heart was pounding like mine, unlike me she was frightened not excited.

b. Construct a sentence or sentence group that contains words expressing relationships of similarity or dissimilarity. For your topic think about *how one experience, person, book, or object is like or unlike another.*

_____

_____

_____

_____

_____

_____

5. a. Underline the words and phrases expressing order of division in the following paragraph.

There are four ways of utterly confusing a term paper project. First, choose a big topic that has forty-five books written on it and one-hundred-and-forty-five articles. Second, read books in which two-thirds of the vocabulary might as well be in High German. Third, time your writing with midterm week, and, finally, give your paper to the typist on the day before it is due.

b. Construct a paragraph using words indicating order of division. For your subject think about *the different kinds of students in your school (or friends, or teachers); the kinds of jobs you have applied for; cars you have owned; sports you enjoy.*

_____

_____

_____

_____

_____

_____

_____

_____

EXERCISE 7   Practicing Coherence through Clear Pronoun Reference

Make the following excerpt from a story more coherent, clarifying pronoun references by replacing them with nouns, adding new pronouns, or using a different pronoun. Mark changes above the line.

Lady Geraldine and the girls reached the great hall where dinner had been served last night which seemed deserted, but as they stood a moment quietly, they saw smoke curling from the cigarette of a figure almost hidden in a chair. They deduced from its shrunken look that it was the elderly aunt of the hostess, Lady Geraldine.

"Please make yourself comfortable," she said.

They sat on the long couch in front her, awaiting her reaction to them. She began to tell them a story, a Cinderella tale about a stepchild who had run away from a cruel stepmother. She had interrupted her flight twice, once to help a woman in trouble and next, a lost child. It had resulted in gifts of two eggs which must be broken when in trouble. The story was long, but they could see that they won her a beautiful gown and a handsome prince.

Politely they thanked her, wondering in the meantime, what this had to do with them in this age of Star Wars. They then wished them a good night and proceeded to the bedroom.

Name _____ *Date* _____

EXERCISE 8 Recognizing Referential Words and Phrases

First, bracket referential words and their antecedents. Next, make a list of the words under their antecedents.

EXAMPLE

The third [stage] of writing [my research paper] was gathering [information] on [notecards] . These [3″ by 5″ cards] contained [limited writing space] , and, as a result, [the summaries] had to be [short] and the handwriting [small] . I filled [many cards] because of the premonition that not [all] would be useful in [the paper] , itself. When I felt that I had [enough] , I progressed to the fourth [step] , organizing the paper.

Stage	Notecards	Limited Writing Space	Information	My research paper
Step	3″ × 5″ cards	Short	Summaries	The paper
	Many Cards + all	Small		Itself / The paper
	Enough			

1. My apprehensions about the newswriting courses began to fade when I met the teacher. He was a part-time professor, but a full-time reporter for the *Free Press*. He ran our class like a newsroom, not a classroom, calling himself the "Chief" and us the "reporters."

_____

_____

_____

_____

_____

2. Over the last few years, jogging seems to have become a part of many people's lives. Jogging is a sport anyone can participate in. Persons from ten to eighty are seen running everywhere, in parks, oh roads, on trails, even in the city. They need very little special equipment, only a good pair of running shoes and sensible clothing. They do need some knowledge of the sport, which should include stretching and striding techniques and relaxation exercises.

_____

_____

_____

_____

_____

_____

3. The *Star Wars* trilogy is based on the life and experiences of the main character, Luke Skywalker. All three of the movies deal with the early background and personality development of Skywalker as this character moves from boyhood to hero status. These developmental stages become the story line of the *Star Wars* saga.

_____

_____

_____

_____

_____

_____

_____

Name ——————————————— *Date* ——————

EXERCISE 9 Recognizing Repeated Words and Syntactical Patterns

In the following paragraphs underline the repeated words and bracket the repeated patterns.

EXAMPLE

Anthropologists record increased tension progressing to distrust and even to hate between people of different languages. [What is unknown,] [what is different] is feared. We are secure among those like us.

1. Out of the suburbs, out of the cities, out of the farmyards came the people— people eager to hear his message. They filled the stadium, singing and cheering, not guessing that they would return to their suburbs, cities, and farms unfulfilled.

2. Did you ever wake up in the morning, roll out of bed, look in the mirror, and notice that your stomach is hanging over your pajamas? I mean that the cute little spare tire you used to carry around with you in your green years had inflated so that you can't see your toes? Well, if you are in the kind of shape that if you pinch an inch, you grab a slab instead, you might be interested in an activity I am very fond of. Running.

3. Feathers, feathers, feathers, they covered the bed, the floor, the chairs, and windowsills. Of course, they had come from those magnificent down pillows I loved to sink down in every night after the late newscast. But who had shredded them and scattered the feathers so wildly about? Not Pudgie, never Pudgie! Nevertheless, there was our black Pudgie as white as snow from feathers stuck to her rough curly hair from her tail to her eyebrow bangs.

EXERCISE 10   Recognizing Ellipses

In the following sentences and sentence group, locate the ellipses in parallel constructions. Write the sentences on the lines below, putting back in what has been omitted.

EXAMPLE

The men had planned on playing hockey, but Matthew wouldn't play, and, as a result, Tom wouldn't either.

> *The men had planned on playing hockey, but Matthew wouldn't play hockey, and, as a result, Tom wouldn't play hockey either.*

1. By ten o'clock, George had come, and so had Sarah and May, but not Leo.

2. Fairly soon, though, I discovered I would have to work to remain in school and also to study. First, I worked part-time and studied full-time. Then I reversed that and worked full- and studied part-time. Now, I am back at stage one, studying full-time and working.

3. We did Saturday's menu first, Sunday's next, and Monday's straight through Friday's in a big hurry.

4. The cultivated rose is subject to many diseases, but the wild rose is not.

5. Marriage is the best of human statuses and the worst.

EXERCISE 11   Combining Sentences into Paragraphs

The following sentence groups when recombined will constitute complete paragraphs. Rearrange the sentences to make a coherent paragraph, and number them in their new order. Look for clues to the paragraph method in the topic sentence; look for clues to arrangement of the sentences in the transitional phrases and referential words and phrases. Item 3 may be arranged in more than one way.

1. TOPIC SENTENCE: There are a number of qualities a social worker must possess in order to help other human beings.

   _____ Finally, they must be able to maintain their own integrity in the face of some very disturbing human behavior.
   _____ They must have patience, a sense of humor, concern for their clients, and the ability to see the inside emotions that the clients are attempting to express.
   _____ In addition, they must be able to accept the rejection of clients who don't understand the value of the help offered.

2. TOPIC SENTENCE: The two ice cream trucks that drive down our block have only the noise level of their music in common; the personalities of the drivers, the goodies they sell, and the music they play are all different.

   _____ He sells all kinds of sweets, ice cream sticks, popsicles, gum, and candy.
   _____ On the other hand, Nicole drives rapidly, challenging the teenagers she attracts to catch up with her.
   _____ Mike drives slowly, making certain that all the children have a chance to catch up with him.
   _____ She sells ice cream, but pop and snacks are her main offering.
   _____ The children gather around, dumping piles of pennies, which he never counts, into his hand.
   _____ The teenagers joke and push as they gulp down the pop even before she starts up.
   _____ Mike's music box plays marching tunes that invite the children into pied-piper parades behind the truck.
   _____ Her music—you guessed it—is loud, loud rock.

EXERCISE 12   Summarizing in Paragraphs—Expanding into an Essay

A. Imagine that you have promised to take notes for a classmate who is absent from your history, science, English, or social studies class. Write a summary paragraph of the points made in the lecture or discussion for the day or days of absence. Be careful that your summary has a topic sentence and that the notes are held together by appropriate transitions, clear references, and other techniques that help achieve coherence.

B. Next, select one (or more) of the points in the lecture and search for information about it in newspapers, magazines, reference books, and your class text. Establish a thesis and compose an essay using the information you have unearthed. Consider this essay as study material for an exam in the course or the beginning of a term paper.

3
BASIC SENTENCE GRAMMAR: WORD CLASSES

Whenever you speak or write, you use the *words, phrases,* and *clauses* that make up sentences. Even though you communicate successfully without identifying these parts or knowing how they function, learning their names, their functions, and the patterns they form in sentences will help you to control their forms and placement.

There are seven basic classes of words: *verbs, nouns, pronouns, adjectives, adverbs, conjunctions,* and *prepositions.*

Verbs (13a)

Verbs function in three different ways: some verbs make assertions or statements about their subjects; some verbs transfer action from the subject to an object; other verbs link the subject with a complement. (For problems with verbs see Chapter 10.)

Transitive Verbs (TV) transfer the action from the subject (S) to the direct object (DO), which usually follows the verb:

    S TV   DO
    We *ate* a barrel of apples.

Intransitive Verbs (IV) make an assertion about the subject. They are not followed by a direct object:

        S   IV
    Nine people *died.*

Linking Verbs (LV) come between a subject and a subject complement (SC) and join the two together:

        S   LV SC
    The grass *is* plentiful.
        S   LV   SC   LV SC
    The water *tastes* fresh and *feels* cold.

The following frequently function as linking verbs: *am, are, is, was, were; become, seem, appear, sound, taste, look, feel, smell, grow, prove, rank, remain, turn out.*

Some verbs can be transitive in one sentence and intransitive or linking in another:

LV
The prospects *appear* good.

IV
The truck *appears* in the distance.

IV   TV   DO
The wind *blew*. The wind *blew* the fence over.

Nouns and Verbal Nouns (13b)

Nouns function to name or identify people, places, things, or ideas (Americans, a park, a car, hope). Verbal nouns look like verbs but function to name actions (to saw, hammering). Nouns fulfill the following purposes within sentences (For problems with nouns see chapter 6):

Subjects (s) are the nouns that sentences make statements about:

S
Children learn from playing.

Two or more subjects joined by *and* make a compound subject:

S   S
The *sawing* and the *hammering* stopped.

Subject Complements (SC) can be either nouns or adjectives that follow a linking verb. Noun complements refer back to the subject of the sentence:

S   LV   SC
The *advocates* of the program *are* young *parents*.

Appositives (A) define or describe a preceding noun. They are enclosed in commas:

S   A
Elizabeth, the owner of a van, drove.

Direct Objects (DO) are nouns that receive the action of transitive verbs:

TV   DO
The new species *could transform* our *crops*.

Indirect Objects (IO) usually precede the direct object and state for whom, for what, to whom, or to what something is done. Sometimes indirect objects are preceded by *to* or *for* and are placed after direct objects:

TV   IO   DO
The starter *gave* the *men* a *signal*.

TV   DO   IO
The starter *gave* a *signal* to the *men*.

Objects of Prepositions (OP) are nouns that follow prepositions (P) in order to complete a prepositional phrase:

P   OP
with squeaking *gears*

P   OP
of the *drill*.

Object Complements (OC) follow direct objects and complete their meaning:

DO   OC
The office personnel found the *boss* a friendly *person*.

Infinitive and Gerund Objects (INF O and GER O) are the objects of infinitives (INF) and gerunds (GER). Because these two forms are made from verbs, they can take objects as verbs do:

GER   GER O
Selling mobile homes is difficult.

INF   INF O
To sell mobile homes is difficult.

Pronouns   (13c)

Many pronouns function similarly to nouns, "standing in" for nouns and noun phrases. Others serve as adjectives marking possession or relationship. Pronouns may be classified as *personal, reflexive, demonstrative, relative, interrogative,* and *indefinite*. (For problems with pronouns see chapter 6.)

Personal pronouns are used as subjects; subject complements; indirect objects; and as objects of verbs, prepositions, gerunds, and infinitives. They are also used to show possession. Personal pronouns used as subject complements are *I, you, she (he, it); we, you, they*.

S
They are wild ones.

SC
The wild ones are *they*.

Personal pronouns used as objects and indirect objects of verbs and as objects of prepositions, gerunds, and infinitives use the objective case. They are *me, you, her (him, it); us, you, them.*

DO   GER O
He seized *them.* He grew tired of watching *me.*

OP   IO   INF O
The man behind *us* told *me* to watch *them.*

Possessive pronouns that are used as subjects and subject complements are *mine, yours, hers, (his, its); ours, yours, theirs.*

S
Mine is the red pop.

SC
The red pop is *theirs.*

Possessive pronouns that signal possession in a noun that follows are *my, your, her (his, its); our, your, their.*

His light went on.	*Our* light is off.
My light is on.	*Your* light is on.
Its light is on.	*Their* lights are on.

Reflexive Pronouns refer back to a person or thing mentioned earlier in the sentence. They are derived from personal pronouns by adding the suffix *-self.* Reflexive pronouns have two common uses: 1) they function as direct and indirect objects and as objects of a preposition when these refer to the same person or thing as the subject; 2) they function as appositives for emphasis or as adverbs with *by* sometimes omitted. The reflexive pronouns are *myself, yourself, herself (himself, itself); ourselves, yourselves, themselves.*

DO
The *earthquake* made *itself* felt for fifty miles.

IO
The *author* found *herself* a new office.

A
They *themselves* caused the defeat.

OP
He developed the new strain of virus by *himself.*

Demonstrative Pronouns point out, define, or indicate how near or far away something is. They may be used by themselves or as adjectives. The demonstrative pronouns are *this, that; these, those.*

S   S
This is bigger than *that* is.

ADJ   ADJ
This watermelon is bigger than *that* watermelon.

Relative Pronouns link a relative clause to the rest of the sentence. They function in the subject, object, and possessive positions within their own clauses. The relative pronouns that function in subject positions are *who, whoever, which, whichever,* and *that.* The relative pronouns that function in object positions are *whom, whomever, which, whichever,* and *that.* The relative pronoun that functions in a possessive position is *whose.*

S
The judge told *whoever* took the stand to be truthful.

DO
The people *whom* the dragon eats are peasants.

POSS
The king *whose* dragon eats the peasants is cruel.

Interrogative Pronouns help ask questions. They function in subject, object, possessive, and adverb positions. The interrogative pronouns that function in subject positions are *who, whoever, what, whatever;* the interrogative pronouns functioning in object positions are *whom* and *whomever;* and in the possessive position, *whose.* Interrogative pronouns functioning as adverbs are *where, wherever, when, whenever, why, how,* and *however.*

S
Who told you?

DO
Whom did you tell?

POSS
Whose is this?

ADV
When did you write it?

Indefinite Pronouns refer nonspecifically to people and things. The indefinite pronouns are *one, all, each, several, many, another, others, enough, few, less, little, much, more, any; anybody, anyone, anything; none, nobody, no one, nothing; some, somebody, someone, something; everybody, everyone, everything.* The pronouns *one* and *-body* have possessive forms: *one's* life or *everybody's* happiness.

S   S
Nobody knew, and *no one* cared.

DO
The crowd heard *nothing* about the tragedy!

POSS
Is this *somebody's* sweater?

Adjectives and Verbal Adjectives (13d)

Adjectives (ADJ) modify nouns and pronouns by describing, defining, specifying, or qualifying them.

> ADJ ADJ ADJ ADJ
> A *reddened* face, *averted* eyes, and *awkward, nervous* movements characterize shyness.

Verbal adjectives or participles are formed from verbs. They often look like verbs but modify nouns or pronouns.

VERB	ADJECTIVE	MODIFIED NOUN
grow	*growing*	*growing* passion
heat	*heated*	*heated* pool

Adverbs (13e)

Adverbs (ADV) modify verbs, adjectives, other adverbs, or whole sentences. Adverbs often end with the suffix *-ly*.

> ADV ADV ADV
> *Fortunately*, the *badly* beaten team *now* had a second chance.

Prepositions (13f)

Prepositions show relationships between a noun or a pronoun and something else in the sentence, and the prepositional phrase functions as an adjective or an adverb in the sentence. Some of the prepositions are *about, above, according to, across, after, against, along, among, apart from, around, as against, aside from, at; because of, before, behind, below, beneath, between, by; concerning; despite, during; for, for the sake of, from; in, instead of, into; like; notwithstanding; of, off, on, on account of, opposite to, out of, outside of, over; past; regarding; since; through, to, toward; under, until, up, upon; via; with, within.*

> P P
> She put her palms *against* each other *on* the table.
> P
> Her shoulders were bent *toward* him.

Conjunctions (13g)

Conjunctions connect words, parts of a sentence, or two independent clauses. There are several kinds of conjunctions, each performing its connecting function in a different way.

   Coordinating conjunctions (COORD CONJ) join parts of equal status. They are *and, but, for, nor, or, so, yet.*

COORD CONJ

The daisies *and* the roses will be pretty.

COORD CONJ

The car is new, *but* it sounds old.

Correlative conjunctions (COR CONJ) work in pairs to form a correlation between two parts of a sentence. These conjunctions are *either / or, neither / nor, both / and, not only / but also.* These conjunctions join parts of equal status, but with more emphasis.

COR CONJ

Either come with me, *or* stop crying!

COR CONJ

Not only the pants *but also* the shirts don't fit me.

Subordinating Conjunctions (SUB CONJ) join one clause with another clause which it depends on for its meaning. These conjunctions are *although, after, as, as if, as though; because, before; except that, even though; if; since, so that; than that, til; unless, until; when, whenever, where, whereas, wherever.*

SUB CONJ

Because Michael exceeded the speed limit, he received a ticket.

SUB CONJ

My husband is shorter *than* I am.

Conjunctive adverbs (CONJ ADV) introduce clauses. They are *besides; consequently; finally, first, furthermore; hence, however; likewise; moreover; next, nevertheless; therefore, thus.*

CONJ ADV

The expedition moved steadily during the day; *however,* at night it had to stop while the men slept.

Relative pronouns (REL PRO) function as conjunctions by introducing a clause that is dependent for its meaning on another clause.

REL PRO

The liquid, *which* ran in rivulets over the couch, came from George's glass.

Exercise Objectives

Recognizing verbs, nouns, pronouns, adjectives, adverbs, prepositions, and conjunctions, and their uses.

3   WORD CLASSES

Name _____   Date _____

EXERCISE 1   Recognizing and Using Verbs

In sentences where a verb occurs, underline the verb. In sentences where a blank occurs, write a verb that works for that sentence. *Reminder:* verbs occur in dependent clauses as well as in independent clauses.

EXAMPLE

The lost children *cried* and *screamed* when they *saw* the policewoman.

1. Martin _____ for a long time.

2. After you repaired the motor, the truck used less gas.

3. Maudie _____ good coffee.

4. Her coffee is good because it is fresh.

5. His hands _____ to tingle from the cold.

6. He stuffed his pay envelope in his pocket.

7. Inside the restaurant _____ the smell of pizza.

8. Mary _____ a slight movement when she looked back.

9. I hated him when I was eight, and now I love him.

10. Quickly, she _____ her coat, _____ her door, and ran.

EXERCISE 2   Recognizing and Using Transitive Verbs

In the sentences where transitive verbs occur, mark the transitive verbs TV and the direct object DO. In the sentences where a blank occurs in the verb position, fill in with a transitive verb and mark the direct object.

EXAMPLES

       TV   *DO*
Aaron hit a home run.

              DO
Mom *places* the ladder against the roof.

1. The Tribe broke the tie in the third inning.

2. Hawkins _____ a triple to left field.

3. Jones threw the ball away on the pick-off attempt.

4. The bad play sent Hawkins home.

5. She _____ herself a new tube of lipstick.

EXERCISE 3   Recognizing and Using Intransitive Verbs

Mark the intransitive verbs IV in the following sentences. Where a blank appears in the verb position, insert an intransitive verb and mark it IV.

EXAMPLE

Our hiking trip *started* at the base of the Rockies. We drove to the Pacific Ocean.

1. We then crossed into Idaho.

2. Sunlight _____ through the window.

3. People in air-conditioned cars sped by.

4. Bob _____ toward the back seat.

5. She _____ to him softly.

EXERCISE 4   Recognizing and Using Linking Verbs and Subject Complements

In the sentences where linking verbs occur, mark the linking verb LV and the subject complement SC (some are nouns; others adjectives). Where a blank occurs in the verb position, fill in with a linking verb.

EXAMPLES

The horses' hooves hitting the dirt sound comforting.

We *are* happy women.

1. In the western novel, the heroes look lean-jawed.

2. Their gray eyes appear steady.

3. He _____ General Custer.

4. The building material _____ aluminum.

5. This _____ Saturday, and I _____ glad of it.

Name _____ *Date* _____

EXERCISE 5   Reviewing Linking, Transitive, and Intransitive Verbs

In the following sentences underline the verbs. Indicate in the blank to the right whether they are linking (LV), transitive (TV), or intransitive (IV). *Reminder:* verbs used as linking verbs or transitive verbs can be used as intransitive verbs.

EXAMPLES

The fish tastes fresh.   *LV*

The cook tastes the fish.   *TV*

The guest eats.   *IV*

1. The driver stops.   _____

2. The driver stops the car.   _____

3. Barbara looks happy.   _____

4. Barbara looks eagerly for the hidden reward.   _____

5. The marigolds grew rapidly.   _____

6. My aunt grows marigolds.   _____

7. Paul ran across the tennis court.   _____

8. Paul ran his uncle's business.   _____

9. A ghost appeared.   _____

10. The occupant of the room appeared frightened.   _____

EXERCISE 6   Recognizing Verbs in Your Own Writing

Write a short essay on one of the subjects listed below with your classmates as an audience and your purpose to entertain or inform. Before you start, narrow the subject and develop a thesis for it. After you have finished writing, underline all the verbs you have used. *Reminder:* dependent clauses have verbs as well as independent clauses.

Something you begged or prayed for, borrowed or stole.
A physical or emotional victory or defeat.
Try it, you'll like it!

EXERCISE 7 Recognizing the Difference between Nouns and Verbs

Using the words in the margin, write one sentence (a) using the word as a noun. Write a sentence (b) using the word as a verb. (Use any appropriate tense.)

EXAMPLE

press   a *The printing press is in the basement.*

        b *She pressed the brake hard.*

report   1a _____

        1b _____

sleep   2a _____

        2b _____

track   3a _____

        3b _____

pool   4a _____

        4b _____

drive   5a _____

        5b _____

work   6a _____

        6b _____

duck   7a _____

        7b _____

paste   8a _____

        8b _____

laugh   9a _____

        9b _____

bus   10a _____

        10b _____

3 WORD CLASSES

Name _____ Date _____

EXERCISE 8   Recognizing Nouns

In the following sentences, underline all words that designate persons, places, things, actions, or ideas.

EXAMPLE

The <u>colors</u>, <u>scents</u>, and <u>sounds</u> surround <u>Helena</u>.

1. To park is an impossibility.

2. The children ate three slices of toast at breakfast.

3. The smell of warm gingerbread permeated the house.

4. A shadow fell between the lovers.

5. Her mind was filled with dungeons and rapier blades.

6. My mother laid the tablecloth on the sand.

7. Slow baking makes a moist cake.

8. Your paper needs revising.

9. Parking is an impossibility.

10. Darkness settled over Chicago.

EXERCISE 9   Recognizing Subjects

Mark s over the subjects in the following sentences. Bracket the verb.
   Reminder: both dependent and independent clauses have subjects.

EXAMPLE

Summer [is filled] with fun.

1. If Don drives his car, we will buy the gas.

2. Politics never changes.

3. Swimming relaxes me.

4. To win brings a triumphant feeling.

5. Josie is jealous when her brother comes with us.

EXERCISE 10   Recognizing and Using Subject Complements

In the following sentences mark the subject s. If the sentence has a complement, mark it sc; if there is a blank in the complement position, fill in the
blank with a subject complement.

EXAMPLE

The reseȧrcher is an avid golfer and a __*bowler*__.

1. Fear and anger are primary emotions.

2. A circular model became the pattern.

3. The new student is _____.

4. The subject of the argument sounds _____.

5. The road looks _____.

EXERCISE 11   Recognizing and Using Appositives

In the following sentences mark the subject s. If the sentence has an appositive,
mark it A. If there is a blank in the appositive position, fill in the blank with an
appositive.

EXAMPLE

Dr. Roberts, a competent dentist, hired an equally competent nurse,
Mr. Chambers.

1. Who is that man, the one in the white suit?

3. The Riley's car, _____, was stolen.

3. Our best pitcher, _____, has an elbow injury.

4. My pet, _____, won best in the show.

5. The street nearest my home, Grand River Avenue, is very noisy.

3 WORD CLASSES _____

Name _____ Date _____

EXERCISE 12   Recognizing and Using Direct Objects

In the following sentences mark any direct objects DO. If there is a blank in the direct object position, fill in the blank with a direct object.

EXAMPLE

Professor Baylor found an unknown insect and a *fossil* .
(DO above *insect*)

1. Bessie has outmaneuvered the director.

2. A child was throwing a _____ .

3. The plumber attached the _____ .

4. The drought killed the crop before he could harvest it.

5. Columbus discovered _____ .

EXERCISE 13   Recognizing and Using Direct and Indirect Objects

In the following sentences mark the direct object DO and the indirect object IO. Where blanks occur in the indirect object position, fill in the blanks.

EXAMPLES

The black hound found his trainer the packet of drugs.
(IO above *trainer*, DO above *packet*)

The heavy rain provided *Alice* wash water.

1. The old artist drew my father a picture of a woman.

2. The boys collected their grandmother some wood.

3. Matthew paid _____ a fortune.

4. The waiter gave _____ a piece of pie.

5. Should we give Jim the book?

6. Mark built his father a boat.

7. I cut _____ some fresh roses.

8. The cat brought _____ a mouse.

9. The catcher threw _____ the ball.

10. Biofeedback gives the patient immediate information.

EXERCISE 14 Recognizing and Using Objects of Prepositions

In the following sentences, underline the prepositions once and their objects twice. Where blanks occur in the object of the preposition position, supply an object.

EXAMPLE

No trace <u>of</u> *dust* rose <u>from</u> the <u><u>road</u></u>.

1. Around the conical base of the cast-iron pedestal, the ivy twines like a loving snake.

2. The letter from Marilyn rests on the right-hand corner of the table beyond the lamp.

3. Light spilled from the _____ over the _____ .

4. Brian put a glass to his _____ .

5. The girls with _____ whispered to _____ .

EXERCISE 15 Recognizing and Using Infinitive and Gerund Objects

Directions: In the following sentences underline the infinitive or gerund once and label it INF or GER; underline the object of the infinitive or gerund twice. Where blanks occur in the infinitive or gerund object position, fill in the blank with an object.

EXAMPLE

INF

The salespeople intend to <u>inform</u> *me* .

1. To come _____ after a hard day's work is relaxing.

2. Saving money is a safe and popular pastime.

3. Can claiming veterans' benefits be done without red tape?

4. Counting your chickens before they hatch leads to disappointment.

5. It is frightening to witness _____ .

3 WORD CLASSES

Name _____ *Date* _____

EXERCISE 16   Using Nouns

Use the following sentences as models. Write a sentence of your own in which you imitate the model. The functions of the nouns you will use have been labeled for you.

EXAMPLE

               S   OP

MODEL: The *people* stood at a safe *distance*.

_____ *The children played for a long time.* _____

                   S   OP

1. MODEL: The wretched *witness* of the *crime* spoke.

_____

              S   SC

2. MODEL: Petty *ambitions* are poor *goals*.

_____

         S   GER O   DO

3. MODEL: *Owning* a *house* brings *problems*.

_____

        S   A   IO   DO

4. MODEL: Her *son*, an enormous *man*, threw *Jane* the *key*.

_____

        S   DO   INF O

5. MODEL: *Jimmy* wanted *to drive* the *car*.

_____

EXERCISE 17   Recognizing Nouns in Your Own Writing

Imagine that you have been asked to write one of the questions for the mid-semester or final exam in one of your classes. Write out the question, and then answer it in one or two pages of writing. After you have written your answer, underline each noun and identify its function on the line above. Make certain that you write on every other line so as to make room for your identifying marks.

EXERCISE 18 Changing from Nouns to Personal Pronouns

In the following sentences, replace the nouns and noun phrases with personal pronouns.

EXAMPLE
Jackie would have loaned the money to Grant.

She would have loaned it to him.

1. Carolyn thought about an old friend.

_____

2. Should Carrie tell Michael about the confidential files?

_____

3. The command control officer had brought the troops in.

_____

4. Three grenades raced by Rashid and me.

_____

5. The men talked about Kennedy and his sister.

_____

EXERCISE 19 Recognizing and Using Pronouns as Subjects and Subject Complements

In 1–5 mark the pronouns s if they are used as a subject and sc if they are used as subject complements. In 6–10 supply a pronoun in the subject or complement position. *Reminder:* personal pronouns used in subject or complement positions are *I, you, he, she, it, we, you, they.*

EXAMPLES
Will we be able to ask questions?

The person reading the Bible is ___*he*___.

1. He will open the conference.
2. The knowledgeable person is she.
3. They are drilling offshore.
4. The mail carrier is she.
5. We must watch the drilling.

6. Are _____ Mrs. Jones?

   Yes, I am _____ .

7. We are _____ .

8. Those girls could be _____ .

9. _____ threw him into the pool.

10. May I speak to Dr. Gilroy?

   This is _____ .

EXERCISE 20   Recognizing and Using Pronouns as Direct and Indirect Objects, and Objects of Prepositions, Gerunds, or Infinitives

In 1–5 mark the pronouns used as DO, IO, OP, INFO, or GERO, depending on their use. In 6–10 insert a pronoun in the object or indirect object position. *Reminder:* personal pronouns used in object positions are *me, you, her, him, it, us, you, them.*

EXAMPLES
        DO
The sailors dumped them.

Jennifer dropped __*them*__ quickly.

1. Please bring him to us.

2. Do you hear her?

3. I walked behind her and him.

4. She walked to class with him and me.

5. Hearing me over the music is difficult.

6. The dog found _____ a safer way around the barrier.

7. She held _____ tightly by the collar.

8. Our instructor wants _____ to be professionals.

9. I couldn't choose between _____ and _____ .

10. To like _____ and _____ should be easy.

EXERCISE 21   Recognizing Possessive Pronouns

In the sentences below, underline the possessive pronouns. In the sentences with a blank, fill in the blank with a possessive pronoun.

EXAMPLE

Yesterday, she and her husband had taken *their* sons to the zoo.

1. "We took our boys to the zoo," said Mrs. Johnson.

2. They spent _____ allowances on cotton candy.

3. How old are his boys?

4. The boat broke from _____ mooring.

5. My camera gear is on your boat.

EXERCISE 22   Recognizing Reflexive Pronouns

In the following sentences, underline the reflexive pronouns and draw an arrow from them to the nouns or pronouns they refer to.

EXAMPLE

David rode his bike around the track himself.

1. My mother gave herself a vacation.

2. The patient decided to sign himself out of the hospital.

3. You can congratulate yourself on your success.

4. Most people prefer not to go by themselves.

5. Running a marathon is in itself a victory.

3 WORD CLASSES

EXERCISE 23   Recognizing Demonstrative Pronouns

In the following sentences, underline the demonstrative pronouns. Where there is a blank, fill in with a demonstrative pronoun.

EXAMPLE

<u>That</u> is the jet flying us to London. *Those* stewardesses will accompany us.

1. We took that luggage. _____ are the souvenirs we bought.

2. _____ souvenir is for you. Those are for my parents.

3. These kinds of problems can be overcome.

4. _____ is a dangerous mixture of chemicals.

5. _____ process could cut costs.

EXERCISE 24   Recognizing Relative Pronouns

In the following sentences underline the relative pronouns and draw an arrow from each back to the noun or pronoun it relates to.

EXAMPLE

The running child <u>whom</u> you caught in your arms is Olivia.

1. Child abuse, about which we heard little a few years ago, is now out of the closet.

2. The pianist who won the Moscow competition is playing tonight.

3. The sport that she finds most demanding is downhill skiing.

4. The debater whose voice is loudest is Beatrice.

5. The truck that overturned has lost its load.

EXERCISE 25 Using Interrogative Pronouns

On the blanks following the interrogative pronouns, construct questions using the indicated pronoun.

EXAMPLE

Who *Who is Helen's boss?*

1. *What* _____
2. *Where* _____
3. *Whomever* _____
4. *Who* _____
5. *Near whom* _____

EXERCISE 26 Recognizing Indefinite Pronouns

In the following paragraph, underline the indefinite pronouns. Where there is a blank, fill in with an indefinite pronoun. *Reminder:* indefinite pronouns ending in *-body* or *-else* use *'s* to show possession.

EXAMPLE

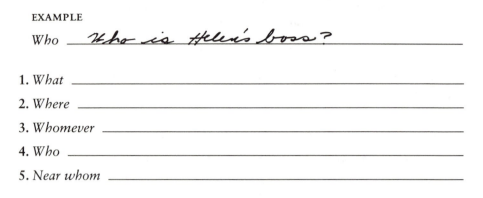

One can say that *nobody's* life is perfect.

She wanted everyone to come back to her camp, but nobody wanted to travel through the forest without something to light up the dark night. "Won't _____ come?" she begged. _____ of them called back, "If you find somebody's flashlight, _____ of us will come."

EXERCISE 27 Recognizing Pronouns in Your Own Writing

Interview a classmate on his or her college goals. From the notes you take at the interview, write a short essay in which you describe these goals. Your audience for this essay will be your other classmates, and your purpose will be to introduce the interviewed person to them. Once you have written the essay, underline the relative and interrogative pronouns twice and the personal, possessive, and reflexive pronouns once. Bracket demonstrative and indefinite pronouns. *Reminder:* in the interview you will want to ask *what* your classmate's goals are, *why* your classmate has such goals, *where* they originated, *when* they were decided on, and *how* they are to be achieved. If your classmate is uncertain about goals, ask about special interests and favorite college subjects.

3 WORD CLASSES

Name _____ *Date* _____

EXERCISE 28   Recognizing Adjectives

In the following sentences, bracket the nouns and replace the underlined adjectives with adjectives of your own choosing. Write the revised sentence on the line below. Don't be surprised if the meaning of the sentence changes.

EXAMPLE

A <u>cool, soft, gentle</u> [song] brings <u>deep</u> [sleep] .

A rhythmic, melodic, sweet song brings sound sleep.

1. They were dressed in <u>Sunday</u> suits, <u>spring</u> dresses, and <u>new</u> shoes.

_____

_____

2. The <u>little-league</u> pitcher rubbed the <u>new</u> ball.

_____

_____

3. The <u>small</u> shoes leave <u>tiny</u> footprints.

_____

_____

4. A <u>tall, big-boned</u> woman was sitting with her <u>seven</u> children.

_____

_____

5. The <u>breakfast</u> smells filtered through the <u>bedroom</u> door.

_____

_____

6. The mayor's reaction, <u>angry</u> and <u>defensive</u>, surprised the reporter.

_____

_____

7. The oasis, <u>green</u> and <u>soft</u> in the dull <u>dawn</u> light, hung on the horizon.

_____

_____

8. Her knee, now <u>swollen,</u> slowed her walk.

_____

_____

9. The child is <u>shy.</u> _____

_____

10. The <u>facial</u> skin appears <u>furrowed</u> and <u>folded.</u>

_____

_____

EXERCISE 29   Recognizing Participial Adjectives

On the following blanks, form participial adjectives from the verbs indicated in the margin. Find a noun for the adjective to modify, and compose a phrase consisting of the adjective and noun.

EXAMPLE

break	Present:	_breaking waves_
	Past:	_broken dishes_

1. _rise_ Present: _____

Past: _____

2. _echo_ Present: _____

Past: _____

3. _corrupt_ Present: _____

Past: _____

4. _open_ Present: _____

Past: _____

5. _stretch_ Present: _____

Past: _____

3 WORD CLASSES _____

Name _____ *Date* _____

EXERCISE 30   Recognizing Adverbs Modifying Verbs and Verbals

In the following sentences, underline the adverbs. Fill in the blank spaces with adverbs of your own choice. Draw an arrow from the adverbs to the verbs or verbals they modify.

EXAMPLE

Approaching aggressively, she _*loudly*_ demanded to meet him.

1. The gulls fly seaward, screaming _____ .

2. The stripe ran lengthwise on the hull of the boat.

3. The sun shone _____ all day.

4. I dislike driving _____ .

5. To run freely with great strides makes me happy.

EXERCISE 31   Recognizing Adverbs Modifying Adjectives

In the following sentences, underline the adverbs that modify adjectives. Fill in the blanks with adverbs of your own choosing. Draw an arrow from the adverb to the adjective it modifies.

EXAMPLE

The *overwhelmingly* sweet smell had disappeared.

1. Big Joseph was always happy.

2. The girl announced my arrival with an annoyingly loud shout.

3. The end of the movie was _____ sad.

4. Her manner was _____ polite.

5. The speech, unbelievably long, sent me to sleep.

EXERCISE 32   Recognizing Adverbs Modifying Adverbs and Whole Sentences

In the following sentences underline the adverbs. Draw an arrow from the adverb to the adverb or the whole sentence that it modifies.

EXAMPLE

Patricia loses her contact lenses very often.

1. Undoubtedly, the mission will be successful.

2. Junior almost never lies.

3. Curiously, I have never liked chewing gum.

4. Jessie nearly always hugs me.

5. They fell rapidly downward.

EXERCISE 33   Changing Adjectives into Adverbs

In each sentence below underline the adjective. Change the adjective into an adverb, and rewrite the sentence using the adverb on the line below.

EXAMPLE
The bus made a sharp turn.

The bus turned sharply.

1. The woman spoke in a soft voice.

_____

2. The witch performed a weird dance.

_____

3. Jim made an angry speech about child abuse.

_____

4. Her song was happy.

_____

5. His shouts were joyous.

_____

3 WORD CLASSES

Name _____ Date _____

EXERCISE 34   Recognizing Prepositions

In the following sentences underline the prepositions.

EXAMPLE
<u>Over</u> the past ten years, an estimated four million Cambodians have been forced <u>from</u> their homes.

1. Controversial moves made by the United Nations in late July dimmed the fading hopes of peace.
2. After robbing their victims, the thugs escaped in a car.
3. Throughout the country, male exotic dancers have become a thriving phenomenon.
4. According to the schedule, guided tours don't start until 10 A.M.
5. Behind the barn near Thompson's plantation is an antique plow used by my grandfather.

EXERCISE 35   Recognizing and Using Conjunctions

In the following sentences underline the coordinating and correlative conjunctions and the conjunctive adverbs. Using the sentence given as a model, compose a sentence on the line below it that uses the same conjunctions in the same way.

EXAMPLE
On my first visit to the library, I found a subject for my paper; <u>however</u>, that was all I found.

Sexism does exist in children's literature; however, recent publications for children are nonsexist.

1. Either mothers were pictured in aprons or little girls were shown sweeping.

   _____

   _____

2. Women were given the role of housewife, but men were engineers, doctors, and plumbers. _____

   _____

3. Now, children's books show mothers as wage earners; moreover, little girls take part in sports and make plans to be doctors. _____

   _____

   _____

4. Public Safety towed my car away, and I will have to pay a fine. _____

_____

_____

5. Not only is a day of worry more exhausting than a week of work, but it is

also a waste of time. _____

_____

_____

4
BASIC SENTENCE GRAMMAR: PHRASES, CLAUSES, AND SENTENCES

Phrases (13h)

A phrase is a group of related words without a subject or a predicate. There are verb phrases, noun phrases, gerund phrases, infinitive phrases, participial phrases, absolute phrases, and prepositional phrases.

Verb Phrases consist of a main verb with its auxiliaries. They fill the same position in sentences that single verbs do.

> SINGLE VERB: She *charged* the battery.
> VERB PHRASE: She *could have charged* the battery.

Noun Phrases consist of a noun or pronoun and its modifiers. These fill the same places in sentences that single nouns and pronouns do.

> SINGLE NOUN: *Evening* passed.
> NOUN PHRASES: *The hot evening* released *a tiny breeze.*

Two special kinds of noun phrases are infinitive phrases and gerund phrases. *Infinitive Phrases* (INF PH) consist of an infinitive subject or object and its modifiers. These phrases function in the same positions as nouns.

> INF PH
> SUBJECT: *To lose them* after saving them was the tragedy.
> INF PH
> OBJECT: He tried *to save them.*

Gerund Phrases (GER PH) consist of a gerund with modifiers and objects. These phrases function in the same positions as nouns.

> GER PH   GER PH
> SUBJECT; OBJECT: *Getting lost* upset *our timing.*

Participial Phrases (PART PH) consist of a participle together with its modifiers. These phrases function in adjective positions, but are usually separated by commas from the nouns and pronouns they modify.

PART PH

ADJECTIVE: *Reeling back*, he fell against the ropes.

Absolute Phrases (AB PH) consist of a noun plus a participle and other modifiers. These phrases function as modifiers of whole sentences and are separated from the sentence by a comma.

AB PH

MODIFIES WHOLE SENTENCE: *The meal not having been cleared away*, the cold coffee still stands on the table.

Prepositional Phrases (P PH) consist of prepositions with their objects and modifiers. These phrases can function as either adjectives or adverbs.

P PH

ADJECTIVE: The flight *for political domination* began long ago.

Clauses (13i)

Clauses contain a subject and a complete verb. Clauses are either independent or dependent; dependent clauses are either subordinate or relative.

Independent clauses function as a sentence or as the main clause of a sentence.

                    S   V

ONE INDEPENDENT CLAUSE: *Monte began the rally by bunting Stan to second base.*

                         S   V

TWO INDEPENDENT CLAUSES JOINED BY A CONJUNCTION: *Stan slid to third base,*

S   V

and Bill stole second.

Subordinate clauses, although they contain a subject, can't stand alone as can a sentence or an independent clause, but always must be attached to an independent clause.

Subordinate adverbial clauses (ADV CL) function as adverbs in a sentence and begin with such conjunctions as *although*, *after*, *if*, and *because*.

ADV CL

When Stan hit the home run, the crowd knew the rally was on.

ADV CL

We can drive into the area *now that the smoke has dispersed.*

Subordinate noun clauses (N CL) function as nouns in the subject and object positions. These clauses usually begin with *that* or *what,* but sometimes the conjunction is dropped and the subject, verb, and modifiers act as a clause without the introductory conjunction.

N CL
SUBJECT: *What they say* is disagreeable to her.

N CL
OBJECT: He says *that the late eighties will be prosperous years.*

N CL
OBJECT: The minister preached *God is love.*

Subordinate relative clauses (REL CL) start with a relative pronoun such as *who* or *which* and function as adjectives.

REL CL
She wound the wool *which she had spun.*

REL CL
The woman *who wove these shawls* lives in Boston.

Basic Sentence Patterns   (13j)

Sentences must have a *subject* (the main word in the subject is a *noun* or *pronoun*) and a *predicate* (the main word in the predicate is a *verb*). No matter how long or complex sentences are, they are bult on three basic patterns, each containing one or more subjects and verbs. The differences between the patterns involve differences in what makes up the predicate.

Linking Verb and Complement

A linking verb links the subject with its complement without implying any action. The complement is the word which completes the meaning of the subject and can be either an adjective or a noun (see 13a). The subject and linking verb alone would be meaningless.

S	LV	SC
Your brother	is	my friend. (noun)
The light	became	dim. (adjective)

Intransitive Verb

An intransitive verb does not require an object to complete its meaning.

S	IV
The lions	growl.
The sun	disappeared.

Transitive Verb and Object

A transitive verb requires an object to complete its meaning.

s	tv	o
The Australians	won	the race.
The crowd	watched	them.

Expanding Sentences (13k)

Sentences can be expanded by compounding or joining two sentences so that they become one longer sentence and by adding single words, phrases, and clauses to them.

By Compounding: Two or more sentences can be combined. (For exercises on sentence combining, see chapter 9.)

The sun disappeared.
The light became dim.
   can become:
The sun disappeared, and the light became dim.

The anteater eats ants.
I poison ants.
   can become:
The anteater eats ants, but I poison them.

By Adding Single Words:

The eggs are white.
The *tiny* eggs are *very* white.

By Adding Phrases (prepositional, participial, and absolute):

The light exposed the dishes.
The light exposed the dishes *from last night.*
The light exposed the dishes from last night *heaped high.*
The light exposed the dishes from last night heaped high in the sink, *no one having bothered to put them in the dishwasher.*

By Adding Clauses:

Martin cooked.
Martin cooked *because he had no other choice.*
We knew *that Martin cooked* because he had to.

Exercise.Objectives

Recognizing phrases and clauses and their uses; practicing sentence patterns and expansion using words, phrases, and clauses.

4 PHRASES, CLAUSES, AND SENTENCES _____

Name _____ Date _____

EXERCISE 1 Recognizing and Using Participial Phrases

In the following sentences underline participial phrases.

EXAMPLE
Challenging Jack to a race, Bill gunned his motor.

1. He pointed his camera everywhere, photographing every activity.

2. Barking furiously, Red strained at the leash.

3. Having studied the directions carefully, Megan assembled her bike.

4. The huge crowd, expecting a win, booed at the error.

5. Burned crisp, the pancakes resisted his fork.

EXERCISE 2 Recognizing and Using Gerund and Infinitive Phrases

Underline gerund and infinitive phrases. In each blank, write a gerund or infinitive phrase.

EXAMPLE

Sitting down and *concentrating hard*, I tried to sort things out

1. To drive takes longer than _____.

2. Working algebra problems is as hard for me as _____.

3. Jumping the fence and _____ are Shep's favorite activities.

4. My mother wants me to go to school and _____.

5. Standing straight gives a better signal than _____

_____.

EXERCISE 3   Recognizing Absolute Phrases

Underline the absolute phrases in the sentences below.

EXAMPLE
The musician waits, his base fiddle resting against the wall.

1. Her shaved head reflected in the mirror, she begins to cry.
2. They spent the day in their garden, Marisa working the soil and Samuel planting the seedlings.
3. He went on from one thing to another, his enthusiasm waning with each new idea.
4. Their six-day session concluded, they voted 112 to 7 to reconvene next year.
5. The children ate heartily, the grandmother beaming with satisfaction as she watched them.

EXERCISE 4   Recognizing and Using Prepositional Phrases

Using the prepositional phrase supplied for each line, compose a sentence that includes it. Underline any additional prepositional phrases that you create.

EXAMPLE
Phrase: *on her lips*   *The smile of a rector was on her lips.*

1. Phrase: *of gently rising roadway* _____

_____

2. Phrase: *from the noise* _____

_____

3. Phrase: *on the gravel pathway* _____

_____

4. Phrase: *against the concrete abutment* _____

_____

5. Phrase: *during the last days of his life* _____

_____

4 PHRASES, CLAUSES, AND SENTENCES _____

Name _____ *Date* _____

EXERCISE 5   Recognizing Independent Clauses

In the first five sentences, underline the independent clauses. In the last five sentences, fill in the lines to make a complete independent clause (sentence).

EXAMPLES

The swelling disappeared after they packed his ankle in ice.

Norman *has hit four home runs this season.*

1. The trainer packed his ankle in ice, and he watched the game from the bench.

2. Although his ankle was sore, he played the next day.

3. If Monte had his way, he would pitch today.

4. Because Kathy was a girl, Stan would not let her play.

5. Batting is not Kathy's strong point, but running is.

6. The catch which Monte made _____.

7. To throw the ball correctly _____.

8. _____ hit the barrier.

9. Skipping our afternoon classes _____.

10. It _____

_____.

EXERCISE 6   Using Independent and Dependent Clauses

On the lines below write a sentence composed of an independent clause and an adverbial subordinate clause which uses one of the indicated conjunctions.

EXAMPLE
where or *wherever*

Wherever you are, I wish you happiness.

1. *after, as soon as, when, until, while, before, since,* or *once*

_____

_____

_____

2. *as if, as though,* or *as; so that* or *so*

_____

_____

_____

3. *in order that, in case, provided that,* or *unless; because, now that, so that,* or *inasmuch*

_____

_____

_____

4. *more than, as . . . as,* or *than*

_____

_____

_____

5. *although, though, even though,* or *no matter how*

_____

_____

_____

Name _____ *Date* _____

EXERCISE 7   Recognizing and Using Subordinate Noun Clauses

In sentences 1–5, bracket the noun clause, and underline its subject and verb. Underline the verb of the independent clause twice. In sentences 6–10, complete the sentence using a subordinate noun clause.

EXAMPLE

[That <u>it</u> <u>is</u> most likely to take place during a period of recession] is one of the paradoxes of rebellion.

1. The reason is that his doctor told him to.

2. A Forest Service spokesman said an observer on a spotter plane reported prevailing winds will carry the ash northeast.

3. The problem was that no one wanted the responsibility.

4. Let us assume that what you do is correct.

5. That I hired an investment specialist has become the subject of gossip.

EXAMPLE
He praised her for *what she had done*.

6. The problem is _____.

7. Maxine told me _____.

8. _____ is what you get.

9. The question is _____.

10. Mr. Meadows will be forced to do _____.

EXERCISE 8 Using Relative Clauses

In each of the following are two independent clauses (sentences). Combine the two clauses by turning one of them into a relative clause.

EXAMPLE
The driver stopped. He plays "La Cucaracha" on his horn.

The driver who plays "La Cucaracha" on his horn stopped.

1. You repeat meaningless phrases. The phrases irritate your mother.

_____

_____

2. The man had been a double agent. Marjorie loved the man. _____

_____

3. Arthur buys oddball gifts. His taste is unpredictable. _____

_____

4. Anna is a single parent. She has two children, and her job is low-paying.

_____

_____

5. The study was on sex roles. On Valentine's Day I completed my study.

_____

_____

EXERCISE 9 Recognizing Clauses in Your Own Writing

Write a short essay that you would like to have published in your school or local newspaper. After you have written the essay or short article, underline the subordinate, noun, and relative clauses that you have used. Your subject might be:

How to find cheap entertainment on or around campus
The favorite trivia now in fashion on campus
A good movie now playing in your local theater

4 PHRASES, CLAUSES, AND SENTENCES _____

Name _____ *Date* _____

EXERCISE 10   Recognizing Sentence Parts: Review I

Write the class and function above each word in the following sentences.

EXAMPLE

N		PRO	N
SUBJ	TV	POSS	DO

The rose   dropped   its   petals.

1. Did you repair the door yourself, or did someone help you?

2. The man who supervises us has resigned.

3. Because laughing relaxes me, I watch comedy on television.

4. and 5. The fruit fly lives a very short life and produces several generations in a year; therefore, it makes a good subject for genetic study.

EXERCISE 11   Recognizing Sentence Parts: Review II

Underline the phrases and clauses and write the kind above each. Underline phrases within phrase or clauses a second time.

EXAMPLE

DEP.CL.   INDEP.CL.   PREP.PH.   PART.PH.

When Mark arrives, Sparky jumps on his lap purring loudly.

1. The weatherman told the merchants to close their stores.

2. After she fell asleep, the fire which she had nurtured so carefully, died.

3. The people who know Anita understand that loving her job is important to her.

4. The once distant thunder now booming very loudly, the storm broke around us.

5. Rustling the fallen leaves with his paws, while he searches for nuts, the squirrel disturbs the quiet.

EXERCISE 12 Using Sentence Patterns

Compose sentences in the linking verb + complement pattern on the lines below.

EXAMPLE

SUBJECT	LINKING VERB	COMPLEMENT
The bell	*sounds*	*loud.*

1. _____

2. _____

Compose sentences in the intransitive verb pattern on the lines below.

EXAMPLE

SUBJECT	INTRANSITIVE VERB
The whole family	*swims.*

1. _____

2. _____

Compose sentences in the transitive verb + direct object pattern on the lines below.

EXAMPLE

SUBJECT	TRANSITIVE VERB	DIRECT OBJECT
My girlfriend	*drives*	*the boat*

1. _____

2. _____

Construct sentences using the pattern indicated at the left.

EXAMPLE

TV + DO *I have finished my homework.*

1. IV _____

2. LV + C _____

3. TV + CO _____

4. IV _____

4 PHRASES, CLAUSES, AND SENTENCES _____

Name _____ *Date* _____

EXERCISE 13   Expanding Sentences with Single Words

Expand the following sentences by using single words. Write the expanded sentences on the lines below.

EXAMPLE

The cook cracked the eggs. *The weary cook cracked the brown eggs.*

1. The doctor jogged. _____

_____

2. The carpenter hammered. _____

_____

3. The nurse injected the antibiotic. _____

_____

4. The technician was a man. _____

_____

5. The balloon grew large. _____

_____

EXERCISE 14   Expanding with Prepositional Phrases, Participial Phrases, or Absolutes

Expand the following sentences by using phrases. Try to use each kind of phrase at least once in the exercise. Write the expanded sentence on the lines below.

EXAMPLE

The rock dropped. *The rock on the window ledge dropped.*

1. The rummage sale was a success. _____

_____

2. The ball landed. _____

_____

3. The van hit a bump. _____

_____

4. The cup was full. _____

_____

5. The paperboy forgot to deliver the paper. _____

_____

EXERCISE 15   Expanding with Clauses

Expand the following sentences by using clauses. Try to use each kind of clause at least once in the exercise. Write the expanded sentence on the lines below.

EXAMPLE

Helen did not sail. *Helen did not sail until she had hired a good crew.*

1. The neighbors have three sons. _____

_____

2. Peter likes video games. _____

_____

3. The bicycle is red. _____

_____

4. The speaker tripped. _____

_____

5. Zachary hugs his teddy bear. _____

_____

EXERCISE 16   Expanding Your Own Writing

Imagine that you are in possession of a secret tape that you have hidden in your house (or room). The time has come for you to pass the tape to a CIA agent who will come to your house to obtain it when you are not there. You must write out for the agent the instructions on how to get into your house and find the tape. After you have made a first draft of this letter, return to it and add details with the help of additional words, phrases, and clauses that will make the location *absolutely* clear.

These letters can be shared with classmates who may want to try to reproduce the directions with maps that they draw from reading your instructions.

5

PROBLEMS WITH VERBS

If you understand the principles of verb formation, you will be able to foresee the problems that may arise in constructing verbs so that they relate clearly to their subjects and to each other. Problems with verbs often exist in the choice of verb endings, auxiliary verbs, irregular verb forms, and in the sequence of tenses in a sentence or a paragraph.

Inflections   (14a)

Each verb has a *base form* which changes to indicate *present* or *past tense,* singular or plural *number,* and first, second, and third *person.*

BASE FORM	INFLECTED FORM
find	She find*s*.
want	He want*ed*.

Present Tense

To make present-tense verbs, the base form is used *un*changed *except in the third-person singular* where *-s* or *-es* is added.

BASE FORM: talk

SINGULAR		PLURAL	
FIRST PERSON:	I talk	FIRST PERSON:	We talk
SECOND PERSON:	You talk	SECOND PERSON:	You talk
THIRD PERSON:	He, she, it *talks*	THIRD PERSON:	They *talk*

In the third-person singular, any singular subject such as *baby* or *chair* functions as does *he, she,* or *it*. In the third-person plural, any plural subject such as *babies* or *chairs* functions as does *they*.

The verbs *have* and *be* have irregular forms in the present tense. The verb *have* in the present tense changes to *has* in the third-person singular.

	SINGULAR	PLURAL
FIRST PERSON:	I have	We have
SECOND PERSON:	You have	You have
THIRD PERSON:	She, he, it *has*	They have

The verb *be* does not use its base form in present tense.

	SINGULAR	PLURAL
FIRST PERSON:	I *am*	We *are*
SECOND PERSON:	You *are*	You *are*
THIRD PERSON:	She, he, or it *is*	They *are*

Past Tense

In order to make a past-tense verb, *-d* or *-ed* is added to the base form in all persons, singular and plural.

	SINGULAR	PLURAL
FIRST PERSON:	I talk*ed*	We talk*ed*
SECOND PERSON:	You talk*ed*	You talk*ed*
THIRD PERSON:	He, she, or it talk*ed*	They talk*ed*

Some *verbs* have *irregular* forms in the past tense. As a result, instead of adding *-d* or *-ed* to these verbs, you spell them differently. (You can find the past tense of the verb you are using, either in the list of irregular verbs in 14a.5 of your handbook or in a dictionary under the entry for the base form of the verb.)

	SINGULAR	PLURAL
FIRST PERSON:	I *was*	We *were*
SECOND PERSON:	You *were*	You *were*
THIRD PERSON:	He, she, or it *was*	They *were*

Past Participle

The past participle can function as an adjective or as part of a verb form. In regular verbs, it is formed by adding *-d* or *-ed*.

push + *ed* = pushed
minimize + *d* = minimized

The past participle of each *irregular* verb has a particular spelling. (You can find the form of the verb you are using in the list of irregular verbs in 14a.5 of your handbook or in a dictionary entry for the base form of the verb.)

BASE FORM	PAST PARTICIPLE
see	seen
go	gone
come	come

Present Participle

The present participle can function as a noun (gerund), an adjective, or as part of a verb form. A present participle is formed by adding *-ing* to the base form of the verb.

push + *ing* = pushing
minimize + *ing* = minimizing

LIE and LAY, SIT and SET, RISE and RAISE (14b)

The confusion between *lie* and *lay*, *sit* and *set*, and *rise* and *raise* can be avoided by remembering the following:

1. *lay, set,* and *raise* are transitive verbs; therefore, they take a direct object:

> DO   DO
> I *lay* the *hammer* down; he *sets* the *hammer* on the table; she *raises* the
>
> DO
> *hammer.*

2. *lie, sit,* and *rise* are intransitive verbs; therefore, they do *not* take a direct object:

> I *lie* down; he *sits* down; she *rises* from her chair.

3. With the exception of *raise,* the past tense forms of these verbs are irregular:

PRESENT TENSE	PAST TENSE	
lie	lay	Note that the present tense of *lay* and the
lay	laid	past tense of *lie* are both *lay.*
sit	sat	
set	set	
rise	rose	
raise	raised	

4. The meanings of these verbs differ:

> *Lie* means *to recline; lay* means *to place something.*
> *Sit* means *to rest; set* means *to place something.*
> *Rise* means *to ascend; raise* means *to move something up.*

Subjunctive Forms (14c)

All of the verb forms studied so far have been in the indicative mood, which is used for ordinary questions and statements. The *subjunctive mood* is used in certain clauses that are contrary to fact, especially after *if* and with the verb *wish* and after demands, recommendations, and parliamentary motions. The subjunctive is formed by using the base form uninflected, *were* instead of *was,* and *be* instead of *is:*

> I demand that he *leave.*
> I wish that I *were* rich.
> If I *were* rich, I would buy a motorcycle.
> The old secretary moved (suggested) that Hazel *be* the new secretary.
> It is important (necessary) that she *take* the job.

Main Verbs and Auxiliary Verbs   (14d)

The main verb in a sentence or other clause, unless it is in the present or past tense, needs an auxiliary (helping) verb. *Be, have,* and *do* are three of the auxiliary verbs:

> The store *is + closing* now. The store *has + closed.*
> You *do + look* gorgeous tonight.

Modal Auxiliary Verbs   (14e)

Modal auxiliaries help express future time or a possibility or condition. A modal auxiliary is used with the base form or one of its participles. *Can, could, shall, should, will, would, may, might,* and *must* are the modal auxiliaries.

Will and *shall* express an intention of something happening:

> He *will come* if you call him.
> I *shall call* him tomorrow.

Can expresses ability; *may* conveys permission to do something:

> I *can operate* a stick shift now.
> Then, you *may drive* my car.

Could, would, and *might* all express a conditional happening and are often used with an *if* or *when* clause:

> I *would* drive if I *could,* but I can't use a stick shift.

Must and *should* both express the need for something to be done in the future. *Must* is stronger than *should:*

> I *must* learn how to use a stick shift.
> Yes, I think you *should.*

Compound Verb Forms   (14f)

Compound verb forms express all of the time relationships except for the present and past. Compound verbs are formed by combining one of the auxiliaries with the main verb to express future and conditional, present, past and future perfect, and present, past, and future progressive.

• *Future* (conditional) is formed from a modal + the base form:

> We *will + install* top-line furnishings.
> You *can + look* at the careful work.

• *Present perfect* is formed from the present tense of *have* + the past participle of the main verb. It is used for an action that began in the past and continues into the present:

> I *have* + *talked* to him many times.
> She *has* + *discussed* her child's health with the nurse.

• *Past perfect* is formed by combining the past-tense form of *have* with the past participle. It is used for an action that both began and ended in the past:

> I *had* + *talked* to him many times.
> She *had* + *discussed* her child's health with the nurse.

• *Present progressive* is formed by combining the present tense of *be* with the present participle of the main verb. It is used with a number of meanings:

> CONTINUOUS PRESENT: More accidents *are* + *occurring*.
> IMMEDIATE PRESENT: Stan *is* + *cooking* hamburger.
> FUTURE: Everyone *is* + *wearing* jeans to the next concert.

• *Past progressive* is formed by combining the past tense of the verb *be* with the present participle. It is used to show continuous action that occurred in the past:

> He *was* + *saying* her name over and over.

• *Future perfect* is formed by combining a modal auxiliary with *have* and the past participle. It is used for an action that begins and will end in the future:

> You *should* + *have* + *used* only one kind of cleanser.

• *Future progressive* is formed by combining a modal auxiliary with *be* and a present participle:

> He said he *would* + *be* + *marrying* soon.

Sequence of Tenses (14g)

Sentences often contain more than one verb, and, of course, there are many verbs in a paragraph. These verbs often have different tenses; it is necessary, therefore, to clearly relate verb tenses to each other in order to avoid confusion. Some trouble spots for writers follow:

1. *With dependent clauses:* When there is a dependent clause in a sentence, the verb in the clause must relate logically to the verb in the main clause.

Often it is logical to make the tenses of both verbs the same:

> She *aims* carefully before she *shoots* the puck.

When the main verb is in the past, use the present in the other clause if it expresses the continuous present:

James *wrote* about why people *watch* accidents.

When the verb in the main clause is past perfect, use the simple past tense in the dependent clause:

The burglar *had entered* because the door *was* wide open.

When the verb in either the main clause or the dependent clause is past progressive, the verb in the other clause should be in the simple past:

Before we *knew* it, the geese *were circling* overhead.
While the geese *were circling* overhead, we *watched*.

2. *With infinitives:* Infinitives usually function as nouns, but because they are formed from the base of a verb, they convey a sense of time. Two forms of infinitives are the present infinitive *(to pull)*, and the perfect infinitive *(to have pulled)*.

Use the present infinitive if its action is at the same time as the main verb or later:

Emily *wants to go* early.

Use the perfect infinitive if its action is earlier than the main verb or if it expresses an action to be completed in the future:

Emily *plans to have finished* her work by April.
It *was* a great feeling *to have finished* my work.

3. *With participles:* A participle usually functions as a modifier or in some cases as a noun, but because it is formed from a base verb, it carries a sense of time. The three forms of participles are present *(pulling)*, past *(pulled)*, and perfect participle *(having pulled)*.

The present participle is used for an action happening at the same time as the main verb:

Talking about old times, they *watch* the sun come up.

The past or perfect participle is used when the main verb is in the past tense:

Having talked about old times all night, they *went* to bed.
Smothered with affection, the new puppy *settled* down to sleep.

4. *With modals:* Modal verbs often occur in a sentence with an *if* clause.

If the IF *clause has a present or present-progressive verb or a present modal (can, will, may), the result clause should have a present-tense modal; if the* IF *clause has a past or past-progressive verb or a conditional modal, the result clause should have a conditional modal (should, could, would, might):*

> If Susan *builds* the house, we *will move* in.
> If Susan *built* the house, we *could move* in.

Do not use a conditional modal with a present-perfect verb in the if clause; instead, use the past-perfect verb alone:

> If Susan *had finished,* we *would have moved* in.
>   not:
> If Susan *would have finished,* we *would have moved* in.

In sentences with an IF *clause but with a noun clause, use a present modal with a present verb, and a conditional modal with a past verb:*

> We *hope* that he *will succeed.*
> We *hoped* that he *would succeed.*
>   not:
> We *hope* that he *would succeed.*

5. *With modals and infinitives: Use the perfect form of either the modal or the infinitive, but not both:*

> Susan *would have liked to finish* the house.
>   not:
> Susan *would have liked to have finished* the house.

6. *In narrative:* The verb tenses used in the main narrative line are either consistently past or present. Of course it will be necessary to use other tenses when the particular ideas demand them.

   In the following paragraph the writer uses *present* tense for the narrative line. When he wants to establish features of his subject that happened in the *past,* he must shift to the *past* tense. When he points to the *future* of his subject, he uses the *future* verb form. He, nevertheless, returns to the *present* tense when he discusses happenings occurring at the time of the narrative line.

PRESENT   (NARRATIVE LINE)   PAST

Sunspots *seem* to hold the attention of scientists. Galileo *was* one of the

PAST

first to see the spots through a telescope. Ellery Hale *discovered* that sun-

PRESENT   PRESENT (NARRATIVE LINE)

spots *have* great magnetic fields. Now telescopes aboard satellites *seek*

FUTURE

more information on the sun. Future studies *will bring* disclosures perhaps

as exciting as Galileo's and Hale's.

Active and Passive Voice   (14h)

Transitive verbs occur in either the *active* or the *passive* voice. In the active voice, the subject acts upon the verb which in turn acts upon the direct object:

> S   DO
> Sonny buries his bones.

In the passive voice, the former object *(bones)* becomes the subject of the sentence and the former subject *(Sonny)* appears in a *by* or *with* phrase:

> S
> The bones are buried by *Sonny.*

The active voice is formed in its different tenses as described in the preceding sections. The passive voice is formed by adding a form of *be* to the *past participle.*

> The ribs *are + cooked* to perfection.
> They *were + served* by the cook.

You should take care that the auxiliary verbs used in both active and passive constructions agree with their subjects. In addition, although the passive voice can be used effectively, the active voice gives a livelier, more forward movement to your prose and is often the preferred voice. (See chapter 9, exercise 16 on using changes between passive and active to vary word order and emphasis; also chapter 10, exercise 9 on recognizing and revising passive voice.)

Exercise Objectives

Recognizing, forming, and using verb tenses; using verb tenses in sequences; forming passive and active voices.

5 PROBLEMS WITH VERBS _____

Name _____ *Date* _____

EXERCISE 1   Recognizing Present-Tense Verbs

In the sentences below, underline the present-tense verbs. *Reminder:* verbs also occur in clauses.

EXAMPLE
Flipping through the pages, the clerk <u>finds</u> his name.

1. My family goes down South every year.

2. Our grandmother and grandfather live in Nashville.

3. We like the way they entertain us.

4. I love the amusement park in Nashville.

5. Come with us and share the driving.

EXERCISE 2   Using Present Tense

In the sentences below, fill in the blanks with the present tense of the verb whose base form is at the left.

EXAMPLE

help   We always __*helps*__ each other.

turn   1. He _____ the envelope in his hands.

know, open 2. He _____ before he _____ it who has sent it.

appear   3. A stamp, his address, and "Mike" scrawled in tiny letters

            _____ on the front.

send   4. Only one person _____ letters to him like this one!

mail   5. Who _____ Mike letters addressed like this?

EXERCISE 3 Using *Have* and *Has*

In the sentences below, fill in the blanks with the appropriate form of the present tense of *have*.

EXAMPLE

My neighborhood ___*has*___ a block club.

1. Who _____ twenty dollars?

2. You _____ four dollars.

3. Linda _____ three dollars.

4. I _____ $5.75.

5. Steve _____ one dollar.

EXERCISE 4 Using the Present Tense of Regular and Irregular Verbs

In the following sentences, write in the blank the present-tense form of the verb whose base is in the margin.

EXAMPLE

grow   My beard ___*grows*___ fast.

have   1. Delmar _____ a class on the third floor.

wake   2. Mother _____ us at six in the morning.

tell   3. My grandfather _____ a story about his grandfather.

go   4. That tale _____ back five generations.

be   5. I _____ proud of my heritage.

have   6. You _____ good handwriting.

spend   7. Oscar _____ hours printing his papers.

offer   8. Sally _____ help to her friends.

appreciate 9. Her friends _____ the offers.

refuse   10. Nettie _____ to help.

5 PROBLEMS WITH VERBS

Name _____ Date _____

EXERCISE 5   Using Past Tense

Place on the blanks the past-tense form of the verb in the margin. Certain verbs such as *need, like, use, stop, suppose,* and *ask* frequently need revision in the past tense. Check these verbs carefully.

EXAMPLE

design   A decade ago, they *designed* hallways without windows.

decide   1. Jill _____ to tell Frank about Ted.

order   2. Frank _____ her to give up Ted.

develop   3. A conflict _____.

admit   4. Last night Ted _____ his crush on Jacqueline.

surprise 5. Jacqueline _____ Ted by crying.

stop, stay 6. A long time ago, they _____in Las Vegas and then _____.

suppose   7. We _____ they would never leave.

like   8. Mark _____ last week's menu.

ask   9. I _____ him if he wanted the same menu this week.

need   10. Each man _____ a truck.

EXERCISE 6   Changing Present Tense to Past Tense: Irregular Verbs

In the following sentences, the verbs are used in the present tense. In the blank space, write the past-tense form of the verb. Use the list of irregular verbs in your handbook or your dictionary to help you find the past-tense form.

EXAMPLE

The rain begins *began* to fall.

1. A three-alarm fire breaks _____ out in the East Terminal.

2. The fire begins _____ in the baggage department.

3. A porter sees _____ the flames emerging from a barrel.

4. The week following Christmas brings _____ a thaw.

5. Mr. Lucena teaches _____ me how to play the cello.

EXERCISE 7   Using Past-Tense Irregular Verbs

A. Insert in the blank the past-tense form of the verb whose base form is in the margin.

EXAMPLE

do   The children ___*did*___ nothing wrong.

bleed   1. My finger _____ all over the floor.

creep   2. The wicked cat _____ under the table.

deal   3. The gambling fool _____ the cards.

draw   4. Buck _____ his gun.

swear   5. The gambling fool _____ .

spring 6. Buck _____ to his feet.

fling   7. The fool _____ his knife.

fight   8. They _____ behind the table.

sink   9. The fool _____ to the ground.

forgive 10. Dying, he _____ Buck.

B. On the lines below write short sentences in which you use the past tense of the verb indicated in the margin.

EXAMPLE

catch   ___*I caught a cold.*___

choose 1. _____

dig   2. _____

hear   3. _____

hold   4. _____

swell   5. _____

sleep   6. _____

throw   7. _____

keep   8. _____

awake   9. _____

feel   10. _____

5 PROBLEMS WITH VERBS

Name _____ *Date* _____

EXERCISE 8 Using *Be* in the Past Tense

In the sentences below use the appropriate past-tense form of the verb *be*.

EXAMPLE

Danny __*was*__ a big child.

1. I _____ the best at building a house.

2. You _____ the best at tearing them down.

3. We _____ at the horror movie.

4. You _____ at the zoo.

5. We _____ brilliant at birth.

EXERCISE 9 Recognizing *Lie* and *Lay*

In the following sentences, underline the verbs *lie* and *lay*. Mark DO over the direct object of *lay*.

EXAMPLE

He lays the responsibility squarely on the individual.

1. The responsibility for success lies with the individual.

2. This generation lays the blame on the last generation.

3. His tools lie neatly on the bench.

4. The carpenter always lays his tools neatly on the bench.

5. Old Spot lies around all day.

EXERCISE 10   Using *Lie* and *Lay*

In the following sentences, revise the verbs. In the blank, write the sentence with the verb revised.

Reminder: lie = to recline
              lay = to put something down.

EXAMPLE
Mom often lays down in the afternoon.

Mom often lies down in the afternoon.

1. The information lays in that incredible book.

_____

2. My lazy brother lays around and watches TV.

_____

3. The newsboy carelessly lies the paper on the porch in the rain.

_____

4. The newspaper lays on the porch in the rain.

_____

5. The problem lays in the area of finance.

_____

EXERCISE 11   Using *Lie* and *Lay* in Past Tense

In the following sentences, fill the blanks with the past-tense form of *lie* or *lay*. In the blank to the left, place the present-tense form of the verb you use.

EXAMPLE
Pres. Tense

lie   Old candy wrappers and paper cups *lay* _____ about.

_____ 1. Muffie _____ her mouse neatly on the doorstep.

_____ 2. The clothes _____ one on top of another.

_____ 3. Who _____ the books on my desk?

_____ 4. They folded the towels and _____ them on the shelf.

_____ 5. The scarf _____ on the wet grass all night.

5 PROBLEMS WITH VERBS _____

Name _____ Date _____

EXERCISE 12 Using *Sit* and *Set*

In the following sentences, revise the verbs *sit* and *set*. In the blank below, write the sentences with the revised verb.

Reminder: sit = to rest
           set = to place something

EXAMPLE
I set here just waiting.

I sit here just waiting.

1. Tim sits the tree in that corner.

_____

2. The Christmas tree sets in that corner.

_____

3. Three blue bottles set in the window.

_____

4. Meg sits a candle in each blue bottle.

_____

5. They set together and enjoy the warm glow.

_____

EXERCISE 13 Using *Rise* and *Raise*

In the following sentences, revise the verbs *raise* and *rise*. Write the sentence with the verb revised in the blank below.

Reminder: rise = to ascend
           raise = to move something up

EXAMPLE
Taxes raise higher each year.

Taxes rise higher each year.

1. A wisp of smoke raises from the chimney of the little house.

_____

2. Aunt Hattie rises her children with hugs and kisses.

_____

3. The wail of a siren raises above the sound of traffic.

_____

4. Mom raises early.

_____

5. I rise the issue at every meeting.

_____

EXERCISE 14   Recognizing the Subjunctive

Underline the subjunctive verb in the following sentences.

EXAMPLE
It is necessary that women <u>be</u> granted the same privileges as men.

1. If the film critic were present, she could give her opinion.

2. I wish that a low-budget movie were in your plans.

3. He moved that it appear on Friday's agenda.

4. If I were on the set, the cameras would roll.

5. We requested that the film director be George Wilson.

EXERCISE 15   Using the Subjunctive

Complete the following sentences using the subjunctive.

EXAMPLE
If he _were to tell me_, I would believe it.

1. It is important that Berthe _____.

2. I move that Dr. Smith _____.

3. Joanna wishes that _____.

4. If Peter _____, Meryl would be happy.

5. We requested that the noise _____.

5 PROBLEMS WITH VERBS _____

Name _____ *Date* _____

EXERCISE 16 Recognizing Modals

In the following sentences, underline the modal with one line. Underline the base form of the verb with two lines.

EXAMPLE

How <u>will</u> your club <u>make</u> money this year?

1. You can sell gadgets on the boardwalk in Atlantic City.

2. You will make twenty cents on each two-dollar sale.

3. You should use a flash if you happen to be in a dark area.

4. The camera must be in focus.

5. I might drop by to help.

EXERCISE 17 Using Modals Appropriately

Place an appropriate modal in the blank spaces. Try to use each of the following: *can, may, could, should, will, would, might, must.*

EXAMPLE

___*may*___ I bring your breakfast now?

1. You _____ go to the shopping center.

2. You _____ return those shoes before Saturday. The store _____

   not take them back if you wait.

3. If I am driving, I _____ take you.

4. Tony said that I _____ borrow his suede jacket, but I _____

   return it tomorrow.

5. You _____ finish your education! You _____ need it.

EXERCISE 18   Forming Past Participles

In the following change the base form of the verb listed in the margin into the past participle by adding *-d* or *-ed*. *Note:* when the base form ends in *-d, -g, -p,* and *-t,* the final letter is often doubled, as in *begged* or *wrapped.*

EXAMPLE

pull   *pulled*

mature	1. _____	use	6. _____
listen	2. _____	admit	7. _____
drop	3. _____	discuss	8. _____
reach	4. _____	generate	9. _____
dominate	5. _____	introduce	10. _____

EXERCISE 19   Forming Present Participles

In the following change the base form of the verb listed in the margin into the present participle. *Note:* when the base form ends in *e,* the *e* is usually dropped before adding *-ing* as in *drive, driving.* When the base form ends in *-d, -g, -p,* and *-t,* the final letter is often doubled as in *beg, begging* or *get, getting.*

EXAMPLE

shove   *shoving*

hug	1. _____	strive	6. _____
sip	2. _____	follow	7. _____
bear	3. _____	sew	8. _____
give	4. _____	write	9. _____
go	5. _____	set	10. _____

5 PROBLEMS WITH VERBS _____

Name _____ *Date* _____

EXERCISE 20   Recognizing Auxiliary Verbs and Participles

In the following sentences, underline the auxiliary verb once. Underline the participle twice.

EXAMPLE
He has finished his homework before the class period each day.

1. The rookie was pitching a good game.

2. Each week the mechanic has suggested that he put oil in my car.

3. This year the farmer is facing another crisis.

4. I have given to the March of Dimes each year.

5. You have used up all the sugar!

EXERCISE 21   Recognizing and Using Present Perfect

In the first five sentences, underline the present-perfect verbs. In the last five, write the present-perfect form of the verb whose base form is in the margin.

Reminder:

I have	We have			
You have	You have	+	Past Participle	=	Present Perfect
He has	They have			

EXAMPLES
The people next door have washed their car.

finish   Rosie *has finished* her term paper.

      1. Failure has happened too often to this team.

      2. Nevertheless, they have persevered and have survived.

      3. The King has arrived in style.

      4. He has traveled in the back of a limousine since he was a child.

      5. The hot weather has lasted long enough.

long   6. I _____ _____ for years to cross the plains.

rise   7. We will start after the sun _____ _____.

ask   8. Sarah _____ _____ several times for more ice.

work   9. The students _____ _____ at the canoe rental for two summers.

break   10. Jill and Bob, rank amateurs, _____ _____ their paddle.

EXERCISE 22   Recognizing and Using Past Perfect

In the first five sentences, underline the past-perfect forms of the verb. In the last five, insert in the blank the past perfect of the verb in the margin.
Reminder: had + past participle = past perfect

EXAMPLE

return   The bad luck <u>had trailed</u> him even after he *had returned* the gold.

1. He had hoped to be home for Sunday breakfast.

2. I had attended the opening of the lion's house more than a year ago.

3. At that time a pair of lions had just arrived.

4. A great river had flowed through the canyon.

5. Its power had carried rocks a hundred miles.

suspect   6. The private detective _____ long _____ that the kidnapping was a fake.

disappear 7. The woman's lover _____ _____ at the same time as she had.

victimize   8. The two of them _____ _____ the husband.

ignore   9. The police _____ _____ the evidence.

find   10. The detective _____ not _____ their hideout.

5 PROBLEMS WITH VERBS

Name _____ Date _____

EXERCISE 23 Recognizing Present Progressive

In the sentences below underline the auxiliary verb *be* once. Underline the present participle twice. Bracket the entire present progressive verb form.

EXAMPLE

Adam [is watering] the lawn now.

1. Robbie is unearthing real gems in her quest for the best.

2. She is searching for the rarest items for her customers.

3. You are hurting my arm.

4. I am going farther than you tomorrow.

5. The same thing is beginning to happen here.

EXERCISE 24 Using Present Progressive

In each of the blanks below, write a sentence that contains the present progressive of the verb whose base is in the margin. Bracket the present-progressive verb that you have formed. Use the subject given in each item as the subject of your sentence.

EXAMPLE

substitute   You [are substituting] for me tomorrow.

communicate 1. We _____

lay   2. The neighbors _____

set   3. The waitress _____

keep   4. I _____

cover   5. The blanket _____

howl   6. The students _____

help   7. You _____

carry   8. We _____

generate   9. The film _____

be   10. I _____

EXERCISE 25   Using Past Progressive

In the sentences below supply the past-progressive form for the verb whose base form is listed in the margin.

EXAMPLE

pick   Kelly *was picking* lint from her sweater.

churn   1. The guests _____ the butter.

sit   2. The host _____ by himself.

lie   3. The cat _____ on the table.

complain   4. The children _____ .

blame   5. You _____ me for not filling the gas tank.

go   6. We _____ all _____ downhill fast.

mumble   7. Patsy _____ always _____ to herself.

kid   8. Whenever I saw him, he _____ the girls.

tell   9. What _____ you _____ me?

lay   10. Robert _____ new sod.

EXERCISE 26   Changing *Could of* to *Could have*

In forming the future perfect, writers sometimes confuse *have* with *of*. The result is a future-perfect verb written as follows: *could of gone* or *might of walked*. In the sentence below, underline the incorrect future-perfect verb. Rewrite the sentence on the line below with the verb revised.

EXAMPLE
The ball <u>might of landed</u> in the sand trap.

The ball might have landed in the sand trap.

1. Katy should of had her baby yesterday.

_____

2. Peter could of come to the game with us.

_____

3. Her boyfriend might of called this morning.

_____

4. The coyote will of caught a rabbit by now.

_____

5. The fuzzy wool robe must of felt warm.

_____

5 PROBLEMS WITH VERBS _____

Name _____ *Date* _____

EXERCISE 27   Using a Logical Sequence of Tenses

In the following sentences, underline the verb in the first clause. Insert a verb in the blank with a tense that logically follows the first verb. Use the verb whose base form is in the margin to the left.

EXAMPLE

stare He tilted his cap and *stared* over his glasses.

respond **1.** When we are in trouble, he _____.

come **2.** His dad wanted him to be a veterinarian, and his dream _____ true.

be **3.** When a horse needs attention, the veterinarian _____ on his way.

give **4.** They wondered why he often _____ money to strangers.

bless **5.** We will remember Doc, and we _____ him.

go **6.** Natalie has some time for herself now that the children _____ to school.

miss **7.** Three weeks from now the fans will have forgotten how he _____ the ball.

buy **8.** Debbie was frying the chicken that she _____.

eat **9.** After Debbie has fried the chicken, she _____ it.

eat **10.** After Debbie had fried the chicken, she _____ it.

EXERCISE 28   Recognizing Tenses of Infinitives

In the following sentences, underline the present infinitives and bracket the present perfect infinitives.

EXAMPLE
The campers were happy [to have gotten] out before the blizzard.

1. It is time to take a cruise.

2. To go on a cruise today is exciting.

3. She has to have started from scratch in order to qualify.

4. Bo is supposed to have tied the gate with wire.

5. She is known to have whipped a rattler with a lariat.

EXERCISE 29   Using Tenses of Infinitives

From the verb in the margin, form an infinitive that is logically related to the main verb in the sentence.

EXAMPLE

go   Aunt Jane prefers ___*To go*___ to New York next year.

teach **1.** The only trick left is _____ our pup to beg.

do   **2.** The first thing we ought _____ was to wash his face.

build **3.** Bill was proud _____ the blue-ribbon winner.

see   **4.** _____ a Broadway show while I am there will be fun.

play   **5.** _____ for the President made Tessie happy.

5 PROBLEMS WITH VERBS _____

Name _____ *Date* _____

EXERCISE 30   Recognizing Tenses of Participles

In the following sentences, underline the present participles and bracket the present-perfect participles.

EXAMPLE

[Having responded] to one question, he refused to speak again.

1. Having fallen across the stream, the tree forms a bridge.

2. The gusher came in, sprouting oil over the men and machines.

3. Having eaten the lightning bugs, the frogs lit up.

4. Having scraped the gum off the bench, she carefully sat down.

5. Sitting on his horse, Barry hears a crash upstream.

EXERCISE 31   Revising Tenses of Participles

In the following sentences, underline the present and present-perfect participles. Revise the participles not logically related to the verb. Rewrite the revised sentence on the line below.

EXAMPLE

Gaining time, the train arrived on schedule.

Having gained time, the train arrived on schedule.

1. Coming in the front door, David left by the back door.

_____

2. Having spoken rapidly and clearly, the commentator reads the news.

_____

3. Explaining the chemical formula, the lecturer can leave the room.

_____

4. Building their two-story house, the whole family moved in yesterday.

_____

5. He finally opened the door, finding his key.

_____

EXERCISE 32 Revising Sequence of Tenses in *If* Clauses

In the following sentences underline the verbs in the *if* clauses. Bracket the verbs in the result clauses. Revise either of the verbs to make a logical sequence. Write the revised clause on the line below.

EXAMPLE

If Ernest <u>is</u> there, he [would see] the problem.

If Ernest is there, he will see the problem.

1. If the machine has broken, he would have fixed it.

_____

2. If Paul would have told me, I could have gone alone.

_____

3. If I run a temperature, I would call the doctor.

_____

4. If Arletta would correct the papers, Jackie will hand them back.

_____

5. If Josephine would have come, I would have told her.

_____

Name _____ *Date* _____

EXERCISE 33   Recognizing Error in Verb Forms: Review

In the following sentences underline the verbs. Correct any ungrammatical forms on the line below. Not all verbs need revision.

EXAMPLE
My glasses <u>was laying</u> on the table.

_____ *were lying* _____

1. She had ask me several times. Going with her would of resulted in a disaster.

   _____

2. My dad play a hymn on the piano every morning, which was something he loved to do.

   _____

3. George were beat fairly and squarely. Beating him fairly, Jim accepted the prize.

   _____

4. My mother be one of my best friends. I would have liked to have given her a party before she moved to Utah.

   _____

5. The coach is laying on the hammock.

   _____

6. You could of ran faster! Why don't you?

   _____

7. If you would have been honest, I would have knowed.

   _____

8. Mark have three sisters who helps him with homework.

   _____

9. They had laid in the box for twenty years.

   _____

10. The attorney demands that I am there.

   _____

EXERCISE 34   Changing Passive to Active Voice

In the following sentences, change the passive voice to the active voice. Write the revised sentence on the line below. For more experience in changing passive to active voice, see chapter 9, exercise 16, and chapter 10, exercise 9.

EXAMPLE
The tree was climbed by the squirrel and me.

The squirrel and I climbed the tree.

1. The mugging was observed by two girls walking to school.

2. The cattle had been driven in by us despite the bad weather.

3. The purple jeans were chosen by Veronique.

4. The campus had been smothered by yellow leaves and snow.

5. Joel's hiding place has been found by his brother.

EXERCISE 35   Recognizing Verbs in Your Own Writing

Imagine that your college newspaper is holding a contest for the four best short essays on one of the following subjects:

The craziest thing that ever happened to me
My encounter with heroism
Growing up in my household

Write an essay for the contest—perhaps the class can decide on the winning essays. In your rough draft underline all of the verbs you use, marking the tense above each one and checking to see that your verb sequences are clear.

6

PROBLEMS WITH NOUNS AND PRONOUNS

An understanding of how nouns and pronouns change form will help you recognize problems you may have with them. Most problems occur with the plural and possessive forms of nouns and with the subjective, objective, and possessive cases of pronouns.

Inflections of Nouns   (15a)

The forms of nouns are inflected or changed to indicate number (singular or plural) and the relationship of possession. Some nouns are irregular in their inflection.

Plural Forms

Most nouns become plural by adding the suffix *-s:*

> One girl is here. Now, two *girls* are here.

In compound nouns, the *-s* is added to the chief word:

> My *sisters*-in-law take sugar in their tea.

Some nouns become plural by adding an *-es*. This usually happens when a noun ends in *s, z, x, sh,* or *ch.* It can also happen when the word ends in *o:*

> The *boxes* are purple. The *echoes* are soft. The *buses* are yellow.

Nouns that end in a consonant plus *y* form the plural by changing the *y* to *i* and adding *es:*

> Your party was the wildest of all the *parties!*

Irregular nouns form plurals either by adding a suffix or by changing the internal spelling of the word:

woman   wom*en*   man   m*en*
child   child*ren*   foot   *feet*

Latin and Greek words form plurals either by adding a suffix or by changing the internal spelling of the word:

A single *index* of economic indicators was not sufficient.
Several *indices* were required to prove the point.
A *bacterium* was the cause of the illness.
These *bacteria* are resistant to antibiotics.

Possessive Forms

Nouns are inflected to show the possessive case by adding -*'s* or an *'*. An -*'s* is usually added to a singular noun. When the singular noun ends in *s*, only the apostrophe is added:

I am afraid of the rose*'s* thorns.
I am afraid of my boss*'* frown.

An *'* is usually added to a plural noun:

I am afraid of the ros*es'* thorns.
I am afraid of my boss*es'* frowns.

When the noun has an irregular plural spelling, an *'s* is used to show possession:

The children*'s* boots were muddy.

Compound Possessive Nouns

When a compound or hyphenated noun is made possessive, the -*'s* is added to the last word in the compound only:

My sister-in-law*'s* shower came after the baby.
My brother and sister*'s* car has custom upholstery.

When a compound refers to individual ownership, both nouns receive -*'s:*

My brother*'s* and cousin*'s* cars have stereos.

Possessive Nouns before Gerunds

A possessive noun is used before a gerund:

Doc's *managing* of the team was masterful.
We disapprove of the team's *giving* up.

Personal Pronouns and Case Forms (15b)

Personal pronouns are inflected for singular and plural *number,* for subject, object, or possessive *case;* and for masculine, feminine, and neuter *gender.*

SINGULAR SUBJECT	SINGULAR OBJECT
I laugh.	She told *you, me, her,* and *him.*
You laugh.	
He, she, it laughs.	

PLURAL SUBJECT	PLURAL OBJECT
We, you, they laugh.	She told *us, you,* and *them.*

The possessive case pronouns are used as noun determiners (words that signal a noun) or as subjects or subject complements.

SINGULAR POSSESSIVE DETERMINERS	PLURAL POSSESSIVE DETERMINERS
My, your, his, her, its coat.	*Our, yours, their* coat (or coats).

SINGULAR POSSESSIVE SUBJECT OR SUBJECT COMPLEMENT	PLURAL
The house is *mine, yours, hers, his, its.*	The house is *ours, yours, theirs.*
Mine is over there.	*Theirs* is next to it.

The following guidelines will help you decide which personal pronoun to use:

After linking verbs always use the subject case for a subject complement:

That man is *he.*

After prepositions always use the object case:

The money was divided between *her* and *me.*

In elliptical clauses (where part of the clause is unstated), choose the subject case if the pronoun functions as a subject in the shortened clause; choose the object case if the pronoun functions as an object in the shortened clause:

Derek is shorter than *I* (am).
Darryl gave more rope to him than (he gave to) *me.*

Personal pronouns in the subject and object cases can be used as noun determiners if the case of the pronoun is the same as it would be if the noun were not used:

We people decided to end the crime against *us* folks.

The possessive case pronoun is used before gerunds:

The instructor admired *her* writing and *their* sketching.

Pronouns used in compounds with and *or* or *should be in the same case as if they were used alone:*

Martha and *she* asked *him* and *me* to go.

Do not use an apostrophe with a possessive pronoun used as a subject or subject complement:

The money is *your's.*
   should be:
The money is *yours.*

Reflexive Pronouns   (15c)

Reflexive pronouns—*myself, ourselves; yourself, yourselves; himself, herself, itself,* and *themselves*—always refer back to a person or thing mentioned earlier in a sentence.

The reflexive pronoun should be used only when there is another noun or personal pronoun in the sentence that refers to the same person:

He gave a reward to Stephanie and *myself.*
   should be:
He gave a reward to Stephanie and *me.*

Demonstrative Pronouns   (15d)

The demonstrative pronouns—*this, these, that,* and *those*—point out or define.
1. *When a demonstrative pronoun is used before a noun like* kind *or* sort, *it should be consistent in number:*

PLURAL   PLURAL   PLURAL
These kinds of problems will be eliminated.

SING.   SING.   SING.
This kind of problem will be eliminated.

2. Them *should not be used as a demonstrative pronoun:*

Them people are my relatives.
   should be:
Those people are my relatives.

3. Here *and* there *should not be used in combination with the demonstrative pronouns:*

> *That there* bat is the one I want. *This here* bat is mine.
>   should be:
> *That* bat is the one I want. *This* bat is mine.

Relative Pronouns   (15e)

The relative pronouns are *who, whoever; whom, whomever; whose; that* and *which*. Problems with these pronouns come in deciding which to use.

1. *Do not confuse the subject and object forms of* who *and* whom:

> SUBJECT: Here is a man *who* will help you.
> OBJECT: Here is a man *whom* you can help.

2. Whom *is always used in writing if it directly follows a preposition:*

> Here is the woman *for whom* you were looking.

3. *Do not be misled by inverted word order or by intervening phrases such as "I think," "You said," or "You ask" when you must decide whether the form should be subject or object:*

> You are the neighbor, I think, *who* owns a lawn mower.

4. *Use* whose *as the possessive form for* whoever:

> No matter *whoever's* books these are I am using them.
>   should be:
> No matter *whose* books these are I am using them.

5. Who *and* whom *are usually used to refer to humans and sometimes animals.* That *and* which *are used to refer to nonhumans, objects, and ideas:*

> The professor which I like best is Dr. Malik.
>   should be:
> The professor *whom* I like best is Dr. Malik.

6. *Remember to place the necessary prepositions before* which *in order to make a clear reference:*

> The economic indicators *which* I have heard much are difficult to understand.
>   should be:
> The economic indicators *about which* I have heard much are difficult to understand.

Interrogative Pronouns (15f)

The pronouns *who, whoever, whom, whomever,* and *whose* function as interrogative pronouns—pronouns which help to ask questions. For help in knowing which pronoun to use, remember that pronouns functioning in subject
positions must be in the subjective case; pronouns in object positions must be
in the objective case. (See also chapter 9.)

Indefinite Pronouns (15g)

The personal pronouns you, it, *and* they *should not be used to indicate an
indefinite subject. Use only indefinite pronouns for indefinite references or revise
your sentence to avoid using these words as indefinites.*

> *It* said on television that snow is expected.
> should be:
> The *weatherman* reported on television that snow is expected.

Exercise Objectives

Understanding the plural and possessive forms of nouns and pronouns; recognizing the pronoun form appropriate to its function.

6 PROBLEMS WITH NOUNS AND PRONOUNS ____

Name ———————————————————— *Date* ——————————

EXERCISE 1   Forming the Plural of Simple and Compound Nouns

In the following sentences underline the nouns. Rewrite the sentences on the lines below with the nouns in the plural form.

EXAMPLE
Kroll made three <u>error</u>, while the two <u>editor-in-chief</u> were watching.

Kroll made three errors while the two editors-in-chief were watching.

1. I have helped out both my mother-in-law many times.

————————————————————————————

————————————————————————————

2. Where did those pest come from? I had to throw away six bucketful of cherries because of them.

————————————————————————————

————————————————————————————

3. While they took their three physical fitness test, we were only on-looker.

————————————————————————————

————————————————————————————

4. We carried two desk two mile for my three sister-in-law.

————————————————————————————

————————————————————————————

5. The twenty passer-by picked up the twenty gold dollar.

————————————————————————————

————————————————————————————

EXERCISE 2   Forming Plural Nouns with -es and -ies

Form a short sentence using the noun in the margin in a plural form; underline the plural form of the word. Check the dictionary to confirm the spelling of words ending in *o*.

EXAMPLE

hero   *Now there were two heroes in the family.*

potato   1. _____

           _____

activity   2. _____

           _____

match   3. _____

           _____

crash   4. _____

           _____

fox   5. _____

           _____

community 6. _____

           _____

piano   7. _____

           _____

lottery   8. _____

           _____

loss   9. _____

           _____

tomato   10. _____

           _____

Name _____ *Date* _____

EXERCISE 3   Using Irregular Plural Nouns

On the lines below, form sentences using the nouns in the margin in a plural form. If you are uncertain of the spelling, consult a dictionary.

EXAMPLE

woman *The women are in white dresses.*

child 1. _____

_____

man 2. _____

_____

mouse 3. _____

_____

hoof 4. _____

_____

foot 5. _____

_____

loaf 6. _____

_____

leaf 7. _____

_____

knife 8. _____

_____

wolf 9. _____

_____

shelf 10. _____

_____

EXERCISE 4   Using Plurals of Latin and Greek Words

On the lines below form a sentence using the noun in the margin. Use the noun in its plural form, consulting the dictionary for the meaning of the word and its preferred plural form.

EXAMPLE

alumna *Mary and Betty are alumna of Mercy College*

phenomenon 1. _____

_____

datum 2. _____

_____

curriculum 3. _____

_____

criterion 4. _____

_____

medium 5. _____

_____

agendum 6. _____

_____

memorandum 7. _____

_____

alumnus 8. _____

_____

bacterium 9. _____

_____

focus 10. _____

_____

Name _____ *Date* _____

EXERCISE 5 Changing *of* Phrases to Possessives

In the following sentences underline the *of* phrase indicating possession. Rewrite the sentence showing singular possession with an -'s or '.

EXAMPLE

The boyfriend <u>of my sister</u> drives the motorcycle <u>of his brother.</u>

My sister's boyfriend drives his brother's motorcycle.

1. The fender of my car is rusting.

_____

2. The temperature of my little boy is 102°.

_____

3. The blue hair ribbon of Mary Tess is untied.

_____

4. The feelings of the hostess were hurt.

_____

5. The cooking of Joe assured the success of the party.

_____

EXERCISE 6 Using the Possessive Form

On the lines below use the indicated noun in the singular possessive form. Include the possessive noun in a short sentence. Underline the -'s or ' at the end of the possessive noun.

EXAMPLE

night   *Last night's disturbance was caused by raccoons.*

brother   1. _____

someone else   2. _____

father-in-law   3. _____

Mr. Jones   4. _____

boss   5. _____

EXERCISE 7   Using the Plural Possessive Form

On the lines below use the noun in the margin in plural possessive form in a short sentence. *Reminder:* some words change spelling in the plural.

EXAMPLE

city   *The cities' mayors sat on the left of the podium.*

horse   1. _____

_____

girl   2. _____

_____

bus   3. _____

_____

day   4. _____

_____

party   5. _____

_____

goose   6. _____

_____

man   7. _____

_____

woman   8. _____

_____

policeman   9. _____

_____

freshman   10. _____

_____

Name _____ Date _____

EXERCISE 8   Forming Plurals and Possessives

Overcoming confusion between the plurals and the possessives of singular and plural nouns can sometimes be achieved by charting them. Fill in the chart below with missing forms, as has been done in the first two lines.

SINGULAR	SING. POSSESSIVE	PLURAL	PLURAL POSSESSIVE
girl	*girl's*	*girls*	*girls'*
princess	*princess'*	*princesses*	princesses'
1. _____	_____	boys	_____
2. _____	community's	_____	_____
3. _____	_____	children	_____
4. man	_____	_____	_____
5. _____	flock's	_____	_____
6. louse	_____	_____	_____
7. _____	mosquito's	_____	_____
8. _____	_____	_____	women's
9. _____	_____	sons	_____
10. _____	_____	_____	classmen's

EXERCISE 9   Using Plurals and Possessives

In the blanks below, insert the appropriate form of the word in the left margin. Make it plural, or singular, or plural possessive as needed.

EXAMPLE

child   The _*children*_ love the snow.

party   1. All of the holiday _____ are over.

thief   2. _____ broke into the office.

brother-in-law 3. Both of my _____ are wealthy.

daughter-in-law 4. She borrowed her _____ vacuum cleaner.

beauty   5. Bringing pleasure is _____ task.

EXERCISE 10   Forming the Possessive for Compound Nouns

In the following sentences supply the appropriate possessive form.

EXAMPLE
President Ford__ and the first lady_'s_ reception was held in the White House.

1. Olivia__ and Cassie__ family is large.

2. The zebra__ and giraffe__ comound was littered with cans.

3. The boys__ and men__s choir was large.

4. The weatherman__ and the anchorman__ salaries went up.

5. Both the *Free Press*__ and the *News*__ readerships increased.

EXERCISE 11   Using the Possessive Noun before a Gerund

In the following sentences, underline the gerund. Supply a possessive noun before the gerund. See exercise 16 for practice with possessive pronouns before a gerund.

EXAMPLE
The __dog's__ limping attracted attention.

1. _____ interviewing made great confusion.

2. _____ inheriting a house was a stroke of luck.

3. The success came from _____ designing unusual cars.

4. The dentist was upset at _____ missing the appointment.

5. My _____ giving me a jade bracelet was a thrill.

Name _____ Date _____

EXERCISE 12   Changing Pronouns to Appropriate Form

In the following sentences, cross out the objective, subjective, or possessive pronouns used incorrectly. Supply the correct form, and rewrite the revised sentences on the line below.

EXAMPLE
It might have been she or ~~me.~~

It might have been she or I.

1. Miriam extended a helping hand to her and I.

   _____

2. You and her are coming in our car.

   _____

3. Will Miriam and him come to see you and I?

   _____

4. Our neighbors and us are going together.

   _____

5. You and me always have to give in.

   _____

6. Between you and I, that child will come to no good!

   _____

7. Either us or them will end up crying.

   _____

8. Have Bob and them half a chance?

   _____

9. The flowers, grass, trees, and me are all out in the rain.

   _____

10. Bill and me went to pick up a case of pop.

   _____

EXERCISE 13   Using Pronouns in Compounds

In the following exercises fill in the blanks with the appropriate form of a personal pronoun.

EXAMPLE

He and _she_ walked backward and forward.

1. You and _____ could talk all night.

2. Two hungry people, you and _____, were in the kitchen at midnight.

3. The unchallenged performances were yours and _____.

4. Judy came in to tell Busby and _____ to get up.

5. His great strong voice reached _____ over there and _____ over here.

6. My children wanted you and _____ to open the package.

7. _____ and they watched Tom and _____ try out.

8. Did Judy and _____ come too?

9. Why didn't the winners shake hands with you and _____?

10. Bill and _____ went to the party store.

Name _____ *Date* _____

EXERCISE 14   Using Pronouns in Elliptical Clauses

Underline the *than* or *as* clause that is shortened or elliptical. Reconstruct the full clause on the line below, changing the pronoun if necessary.

EXAMPLE

The note didn't bother Ariel as much <u>as him.</u>

as it bothered him.

1. Soapy makes the children laugh harder than us.

_____

2. Soapy made the children laugh harder than we.

_____

3. Yolanda had to concentrate more than he.

_____

4. The bear found the garbage faster than they.

_____

5. The bear ate the garbage faster than them.

_____

EXERCISE 15   Using Personal Pronouns as Noun Determiners

In the following sentences, use an appropriate personal pronoun as a noun determiner for emphasis.

EXAMPLE

The largest group, __*we*__ voters, went ahead.

1. _____ people make up the electorate.

2. The members of the electorate most important to _____ candidates are you.

3. _____ students are the backbone of the University.

4. The University couldn't exist without _____ students.

5. _____ store owners must absorb the cost of shoplifting.

EXERCISE 16   Using a Possessive Pronoun before a Gerund

In sentences 1–5, insert a possessive pronoun in the blank preceding the gerund. On lines 6–10, rewrite the five sentences using a possessive noun before the gerund.

EXAMPLE

Your hitting a home run saved the game.

Jane's hitting a home run saved the game.

1. Don't criticize _____ catching!

2. _____ glaring at them won't stop _____ asking questions.

3. _____ bungling lost us the contract.

4. A major bureaucratic error was _____ paying bills twice.

5. _____ having worked as a geologist gave her an advantage.

6. _____

_____

7. _____

_____

8. _____

_____

9. _____

_____

10. _____

6 PROBLEMS WITH NOUNS AND PRONOUNS ___

Name _____ *Date* _____

EXERCISE 17 Using Personal Pronouns

Underline the appropriate form of the personal pronoun.

EXAMPLE
Buddy and (I / me) started a revolution.

1. (Me / My) holding on saved his life.

2. Give (us / we) students some help!

3. (Them / They) are the wrong ones.

4. Janice came with (he / him) and (I / me).

5. (You / Your) jogging sets a good example for (myself / me).

6. Those men on the diamond are (them / they).

7. The singers treated the dancer better than he treated (they / them).

8. (We / Us) parents are the guilty ones.

9. I am (she / her).

10. My father and (I / me) worked on it all weekend.

EXERCISE 18 Using Reflexive Pronouns

Use a reflexive pronoun only where appropriate in the sentences below. If a reflexive pronoun is not allowable, insert an acceptable pronoun. Draw an arrow from the reflexive pronoun to the noun to which it refers.

EXAMPLE
Pamela handed the baby to me *herself*.

1. I treated _____ to a hot-fudge sundae.

2. The judge awarded the prize to _____.

3. George cut down the tree _____.

4. The family saw _____ deplane.

5. The students conducted the class all by _____.

EXERCISE 19   Using Demonstrative Pronouns

In the following sentences choose the appropriate demonstrative pronoun. On the line below, write the sentence using the selected pronoun.

EXAMPLE
(Them there / Those) parts have to be packed.

Those parts have to be packed.

1. (Them / These) are the wrong ones. (This kind / These kinds) of nail won't fit.

2. (This sort / These sorts) of toys sell fast.

3. (Them / These) people went to the wrong house.

4. (These kind / These kinds) of wrenches won't work.

5. (This here / This) is the key to (that / that there) lock.

6 PROBLEMS WITH NOUNS AND PRONOUNS ___

Name _____ *Date* _____

EXERCISE 20 Recognizing Relative Pronouns as Subjects of Clauses

Underline the relative clause and bracket the relative pronoun subject of the clause.

EXAMPLE
We began talking about Jan [who] is in Bucharest.

1. Jan will go to Athens, which is a beautiful city that she loves.

2. I choose whichever is the fastest way home.

3. The experiment was conducted on ninety-three students who were taking the study-skills course.

4. Most of the women were busily watching whoever came in the door.

5. He was the man who, I think, arrived last week.

EXERCISE 21 Recognizing Relative Pronouns as Objects or Possessives

Underline the relative clause, and bracket the relative pronoun which is an object or a possessive in the clause.

EXAMPLES
The person [whose] shadow I saw was Arthur.

Millie looked away from the man [whom] Clara had introduced.

1. The person of whom you speak is my brother.

2. She swallowed the milk which Elsa had prepared for her.

3. Clara, whose affairs mature rapidly, was already through with him.

4. The thirty-one students whom he assigned at random were the control group.

5. How could she ignore a man to whom she had given her heart a month ago?

EXERCISE 22   Using Relative Pronouns

In the following sentences, place an appropriate relative pronoun in the blank.

EXAMPLE

Water _*That*_ makes no noise is stagnant.

1. The farmer _____ crops are abundant is happy.

2. He is a man _____ avoids posturing in public.

3. Grandmother had one grandchild to _____ she gave all her love.

4. She left all her belongings to _____ wanted them.

5. Carrie is the friend _____ she asked to stay all night.

6. Carrie is the friend _____, I think, stayed last night.

7. I love the summer days _____ bring me sixteen hours of daylight.

8. She asked _____ books these are.

9. Robert, _____ he had always admired, was not even honest.

10. _____ are you going to the show with?

Name ——————————————— *Date* ————

EXERCISE 23 Changing Relative Pronouns to Appropriate Forms

In the sentences below, underline the relative pronouns. Write the sentence with the pronoun revised on the line below. *Reminder:* the possessive form of the relative pronoun is *whose* not *who's.*

EXAMPLE
I don't know who's dog that is.

I don't know whose dog that is.

1. They never told me whom he was.

———————————————————————

2. The child whom, I think, is lost is over there.

———————————————————————

3. The employee who's success story you just heard is Schmidt.

———————————————————————

4. The golfer who I admire the most is my mother.

———————————————————————

5. Who's child are you?

———————————————————————

EXERCISE 24 Using Necessary Prepositions with *which* Clauses

The following sentences are confusing because a preposition has been left out preceding a relative clause. Write the revised sentence on the line below, and underline the necessary preposition and the relative clause. Include commas where they are needed.

EXAMPLE
I was an outsider which I was treated like dirt.

I was an outsider for which I was treated like dirt.

1. He must choose a subject which he has a sufficient amount of information.

———————————————————————

———————————————————————

2. I found my sweeper's job was one of the best unskilled jobs, which there are

not many. ——————————————————

3. She spoke on a topic which she knew nothing. _____

_____

4. There are ways which our city can be improved. _____

_____

5. The car, the bumper which is cracked, is in the lot. _____

_____

EXERCISE 25   Correcting Nouns and Pronouns in Your Own Writing

Write a letter to an advice columnist asking for help with a real or fictional problem. Exchange your letter with a classmate, and write a letter of advice in response to his or her letter. Share letters and answers with other members of your class. Check to make certain that noun endings and pronoun forms are accurate in your letter and in the response from your classmate.

7

PROBLEMS WITH AGREEMENT

Writing requires agreement between verbs and their subjects and pronouns and their antecedents. The agreement between these parts of speech helps hold writing together, making it clear to the reader what subject the verb refers back to and what noun (or pronoun) a pronoun refers back to. Problems in agreement make these references confusing.

General Rules of Agreement (16a)

Agreement of Subject and Verb

A *subject* and its *verb* agree in *number*. If the subject is plural, the verb must also be plural; if the subject is singular, the verb must also be singular:

SINGULAR SUBJECT	SINGULAR VERBS
The <u>puppy</u>	<u>stops</u> crying and <u>goes</u> to sleep.

PLURAL SUBJECT	PLURAL VERBS
The <u>puppies</u>	<u>stop</u> crying and <u>go</u> to sleep.

Agreement of Pronoun and Antecedent: Number and Person

A *pronoun* and its *antecedents* agree in *number* and *person:*

SINGULAR	SINGULAR
The <u>cow</u> switches	<u>her</u> tail.

PLURAL	PLURAL
The <u>cows</u> switch	<u>their</u> tails.

A *pronoun* and its *antecedents* agree in *gender:*

MASCULINE	MASCULINE
The <u>bull</u> lowers	<u>his</u> head.

When the gender of the antecedent is unknown, follow one of these suggestions:

· Use *her or his* or *she or he* to refer back to the antecedent:

> A <u>violinist</u> takes good care of <u>his or her</u> violin.

· Make the subject or antecedent plural to avoid the awkwardness of *his or her:*

> <u>Violinists</u> take good care of <u>their</u> violins.

· Revise the sentence so as to eliminate the compound pronoun:

> A <u>violin</u> must be well cared for by <u>its</u> owner.

Special Agreement Problems   (16b)

Agreement with Compound Subjects

When a compound subject is joined with *and,* use a plural verb and a plural pronoun to agree with the compound subject:

COMPOUND SUBJECT	PLURAL VERB AND PRONOUN
<u>Brad</u> and <u>Brian</u>	<u>are pooling their</u> resources.

If the compound subject or antecedent is singular in meaning, use a singular verb and pronoun if both parts of the compound are singular:

SINGULAR SUBJECT · SINGULAR VERB AND PRONOUN

<u>My boss and best friend</u> always <u>loans</u> me <u>his</u> golf clubs.

If the compound or antecedent is preceded by *every* or *each,* use a singular verb and a singular pronoun:

SINGULAR VERB AND PRONOUN · EVERY

<u>Every city and county</u> <u>has</u> a responsibility to <u>its</u> taxpayers.

When a compound subject or antecedent is joined with *or* or *nor,* use a singular verb or pronoun if both parts of the compound are singular:

COMPOUND SINGULAR · SINGULAR VERB AND PRONOUN

<u>Mother or Aunt Meg</u> always <u>brings</u> <u>her</u> dishes.

If both parts of the subject or antecedent are plural, use a plural verb or pronoun:

COMPOUND PLURAL · PLURAL VERB AND PRONOUN

Neither <u>the plants</u> nor <u>the flowers</u> by <u>themselves</u> <u>are</u> showy enough.

If one member of the subject or antecedent is singular and one plural, make the verb or pronoun agree with the nearest one:

COMPOUND SINGULAR VERB
SINGULAR AND PRONOUN
Neither <u>the plants</u> nor <u>the flower</u> by <u>itself</u> <u>is</u> showy enough.

Agreement with Collective Nouns

Use a singular verb or a singular pronoun with a collective subject or antecedent. Some collective nouns are *youth, army, police, hair, seed, dozen, score, group, team, faculty, committee, administration.* (If these nouns are preceded by *many, few, these* or *those,* or a plural number, they are plural.)

COLLECTIVE SINGULAR VERB
NOUN AND PRONOUN
The <u>faculty</u> <u>has</u> received <u>its</u> pay raise.

COLLECTIVE NOUN PLURAL VERB
WITH MANY AND PRONOUN
<u>Many police</u> <u>have</u> exercised <u>their</u> rights.

Agreement with Plural-Form Nouns

Nouns that appear to be plural in form but are singular in meaning take a singular verb or pronoun. Some of these nouns are *measles, athletics, politics, United States, mathematics, means, news.* The title of a book also takes a singular verb and pronoun:

PLURAL FORM SINGULAR VERB
NOUN AND PRONOUN
The <u>news</u> <u>itself</u> <u>is</u> good.

BOOK SINGULAR
TITLE VERB
<u>The First Years</u> <u>is</u> a good book for new mothers.

Agreement with Foreign Plurals

If foreign plurals do not resemble English plurals, be certain to use verbs and pronouns that agree with them:

FOREIGN PLURAL VERB
PLURAL AND PRONOUN
The <u>data</u> <u>are</u> not in <u>themselves</u> sufficient.

Agreement with Indefinite Pronouns

Use a singular verb and pronoun when the subject or antecedent is an indefinite pronoun:

INDEFINITE   SINGULAR VERB

PRONOUN   AND PRONOUN

<u>Somebody</u> <u>is</u> blowing <u>his or her</u> horn.

<u>Neither</u> <u>is</u> acceptable.

Certain indefinite pronouns may take either singular or plural verbs or pronouns depending on whether they refer to an amount of something that is not countable *(rain)* or a number of things that are countable *(raindrops):*

NOT   SINGULAR VERB

COUNTABLE   AND PRONOUN

<u>Some</u> of the rain <u>has</u> forced <u>its</u> way through the tent.

PLURAL VERB

COUNTABLE   AND PRONOUN

<u>Some</u> of the raindrops <u>have</u> forced <u>their</u> way through the tent.

Agreement with Prepositional Phrases

If a prepositional phrase comes between a subject and its verb or a pronoun and its antecedent, usually you can ignore it in deciding whether to use a singular or plural verb or pronoun:

SINGULAR   SINGULAR

SUBJECT   VERB

<u>None</u> of the photographs <u>was</u> a masterpiece.

<u>Edna</u>, along with two other girls, <u>goes</u> skating.

Agreement with Relative Clauses

The verbs in relative clauses agree with the nouns that the clauses modify:

We watched the <u>woman</u> who <u>was</u> training to be an astronaut.

Agreement with Linking Verbs

In a sentence with a linking verb, the verb agrees with the subject, not the subject complement:

PLURAL

SUBJECT LV   SC

The twenty-watt <u>bulbs</u> <u>were</u> the only source of light.

SINGULAR

SUBJECT   LV   SC

The only <u>source</u> of light <u>was</u> two twenty-watt bulbs.

Exercise Objectives

Recognizing agreement between subjects and verbs and pronouns and antecedents; recognizing common problems in agreement.

7 PROBLEMS WITH AGREEMENT _____

Name _____ *Date* _____

EXERCISE 1   Recognizing Subjects and Their Verbs

In the following sentences, underline the subject or subjects of the sentences once. Underline their verb or verbs twice, and draw an arrow from the verb back to the subject. *Reminder:* subjects and verbs occur within clauses as well as in the main part of the sentence.

EXAMPLE

The pigeons take off when the cyclists roar through them.

1. The light was green, and I had the right of way.

2. I speed up as the man fires a shot at the car.

3. A Saturday night special was used in the shooting.

4. My brother has to pay an adult fare because he is twelve.

5. Worry makes me old before my time.

EXERCISE 2   Using Verbs in Agreement with Their Subjects

In the following sentences, underline the subject once and fill in the blank with the present-tense form of the verb listed to the left. *Reminder:* in the present-tense third-person singular, *-s* or *-es* is added to the base form of regular verbs; *have* becomes *has,* and *be* becomes *is.* In the third-person plural, *be* becomes *are.*

EXAMPLE

keep   They __*keep*__ their soft drinks on ice.

use   1. Heavy trucks _____ our street.

plan   2. Melissa _____ each meeting carefully.

prove   3. These statistics _____ my point.

seem   4. The economy _____ stable.

have   5. The stove _____ a self-cleaning oven.

EXERCISE 3 Looking for Agreement between Verbs and Subjects

In the following paragraphs, underline the verbs and draw arrows to their subjects. If the verb is not in agreement, write the corrected form above it. In the blanks write an auxiliary verb that agrees with the subject. *Reminder:* verbs in clauses also have subjects.

EXAMPLE

Students _have_ always wanted to enter our

competition because it *offers* offer them a chance to

publish their writing in the school newspaper.

Our contest publishes the winning entries in the *College Herald*. In addition, the town newspaper print the pieces with the most journalistic appeal. In the past the English Department ＿＿＿＿＿＿ received about ninety entries, and five of these ＿＿＿＿＿＿ published in the *College Herald*. Monday and Tuesday, April 12 and 13, are the dates of submission for the next contest.

The rules of the contest is as follows:

1. Entrants has to be enrolled in the college.

2. Poetry, short stories, or essays ＿＿＿＿＿＿ submitted.

3. Only typed or word-processed manuscripts ＿＿＿＿＿＿ accepted.

4. The English Department office handle the admission forms and accept the manuscripts. (The submission form have blanks for a pseudonym as well as for the student's name. Only the pseudonym ＿＿＿＿＿＿ typed on the manuscript.) The first reading of manuscripts ＿＿＿＿＿＿ done by English department members; the final evaluations ＿＿＿＿＿＿ made by a magazine editor and a newspaper journalist.

Name _____ *Date* _____

EXERCISE 4   Recognizing the Antecedents of Pronouns

In the following sentences or sentence groups, underline the pronouns which have antecedents twice. Underline the antecedents once, and draw an arrow from each pronoun to its antecedent.

EXAMPLE

Mr. Roland accused Mr. and Mrs. Jones of exaggerating their case. He said that his child had not even stepped on their lawn.

1. The Cozy Cafe has just advertised its special for the week. It is serving thirteen diet-wrecking varieties of pie on Friday. They are so good you will be tempted to try them all.

2. Thin may be in for most folks, but for George and Bill it was a way out of a tight situation. They wormed their way through a one-foot-square opening in a stalled elevator.

3. Tracy showed her courage by speaking out, but it will probably cost her her job.

4. Bates was lonely on Saturday nights, so computer dating services looked tempting. But instinctively he knew they were not for him.

5. Foot travelers crossing an urban expressway take their lives lightly. They are courting disaster.

EXERCISE 5   Using Pronouns to Refer to Antecedents

In the following sentences supply an appropriate pronoun in the blank space. The antecedent has been underlined for you.

EXAMPLE
Twentieth-century heroes in modern novels try to achieve power by using

their scientific or psychological knowledge.

1. When modern children write _____ own stories and songs, _____ replace magic with modern technology.

2. Only after the writer reaches adolescence, do _____ characters become interested in sex and marriage.

3. I can cope with ugly <u>scenes,</u> bad <u>odors,</u> and poor <u>food</u>; _____ don't

bother me. But place me where the <u>noise</u> is loud and jumbled and _____

will drive me crazy.

4. I was ushered through double <u>doors</u> into a tunnel. _____ clicked

shut and I faced darkness.

5. A <u>person</u> must help _____ as best _____ can.

EXERCISE 6   Changing Pronouns to Agree with Antecedents

In the following sentence or sentence group, underline pronouns twice. Underline antecedents once. Change pronouns that do not agree with antecedents to
an appropriate form. Write the pronouns above the ones they will replace.

EXAMPLE

his or her

The <u>student</u> will soon realize that <u>their</u> writing assignments continue into

the working world.

1. A member of the armed forces must pitch their own tent.

2. Some want to keep our lands unspoiled. Some want to exploit it.

3. The scientist in the lab must ask themselves some questions. For example,

to what extent is their research justified?

4. There is a possibility that asbestos particles cause lung cancer since it irri-

tates the lining of the lung.

5. A student's lawyer must be prepared to lower their fees so as to match the

student's income. Their reward will be the student's appreciation.

EXERCISE 7   Using Verbs and Pronouns with Compound Subjects and Antecedents

In the following sentences, fill in the single blank with the present-tense form of the verb in the margin and place a pronoun in the double blank. *Reminder:* In some cases compound subjects have singular meanings.

EXAMPLE

give   Arts and crafts classes and team sports *give* *their* par-

ticipants a chance to socialize.

be   1. Pigeons and starlings gathering about the house _____ a

nuisance because _____ _____ noisy and messy.

save   2. Because Betty and Joe _____ carefully, _____ will

be able to buy _____ first home next year.

add   3. The stage curtain with its dark velvet trimmings and the back-

drop with its classical figures _____ _____ own pecu-

liar elegance.

receive 4. Each catcher and pitcher _____ a handshake.

lie   5. Every fork, knife, and spoon _____ in _____

proper place.

love   6. Voltaire and I _____ coffee on _____ break.

come   7. The bride and her father _____ slowly down the aisle

have   8. Each woman and man _____ a duty to _____

country.

bring   9. Every virtue _____ _____ own rewards.

cook   10. The father and daughter _____ for _____.

EXERCISE 8   Practicing Agreement with *Either / Or* and *Neither / Nor*

In the following, place in the single blanks the present-tense form of the verb in the margin. Place an appropriate form of the pronoun in the double blanks.

EXAMPLE

be   Either a discount fare or weekend packages _____*are*_____ worth _____*Their*_____ asking price.

see   **1.** Neither mother nor grandmother _____ _____ as a baby-sitter.

be   **2.** Neither the shingles nor the roofer _____ here.

suit   **3.** Either the black blouse or the gray sweater _____ the occasion.

help   **4.** Neither the new battery nor new brakes _____.

have   **5.** Either the two men or the woman _____ the money.

Name ─────────────────────── *Date* ─────────

EXERCISE 9   Using Collective and Plural-Form Nouns

Complete the following sentences using the collective noun given as the subject of a sentence. Supply present-tense verbs and appropriate pronouns where needed. Underline the verb and pronouns agreeing with the subject. *Reminders:* 1) collective nouns become plural if preceded by *those, these, many, two,* etc.; 2) certain foreign nouns have a plural ending *a.*

EXAMPLE

These youth *are the brightest sixteen-year-olds as shown by their test scores.*

1. Mathematics ────────────────────

   ────────────────────────

2. His data ──────────────────────

   ────────────────────────

3. The freshman class ─────────────────

   ────────────────────────

4. Politics ───────────────────────

   ────────────────────────

5. These faculty ─────────────────────

   ────────────────────────

6. The group ──────────────────────

   ────────────────────────

7. Many youth ─────────────────────

   ────────────────────────

8. The sales staff ───────────────────

   ────────────────────────

9. The bacteria ─────────────────────

   ────────────────────────

10. *Little Women* ───────────────────

   ────────────────────────

EXERCISE 10   Recognizing and Using Agreement with Indefinite Pronouns

In the sentences below, fill in the single blanks with a present-tense verb and the double blanks with a pronoun. *Reminder:* many indefinite pronouns take a singular verb and pronoun reference.

EXAMPLE

Each of the women *has brought* *her* child.

1. Everybody _____ here.

2. Another of the boys _____ _____ dog.

3. Some of his anger has left _____ mark on him.

4. Neither of the cats ever lost _____ fur.

5. _____ anyone lost _____ lipstick?

EXERCISE 11   Using Plural Indefinite Pronouns

On the following blanks, complete the sentences using present-tense verbs or verbs with auxiliaries. Underline verbs and pronouns that agree with the indefinite pronoun subject.

EXAMPLE

Many *are here to help themselves.*

1. Several of the tulip bulbs _____

_____

2. All of the skiiers _____

_____

3. All of the skiing _____

_____

4. Some _____

_____

5. Many _____

_____

7 PROBLEMS WITH AGREEMENT ───────────

Name ─────────────────────────── *Date* ───────────

EXERCISE 12   Using Verbs and Pronouns Separated from Subject or Antecedent by a Prepositional Phrase

In the sentences below, fill in the single blanks with an appropriate verb (or auxiliary) and the double blanks with a pronoun.

EXAMPLE

One of the women ___*has*___ lost ___*her*___ glasses.

1. Examples of the art works of the Vikings ─────────── preserved in the

   British Museum where ───────────can be seen by all.

2. From ───────────own earnings, a group of students ───────────

   financing ───────────trip to France.

3. The rescue of the Haitians ─────────── partly successful.

4. A pilot of these home-built airplanes must fly by the seat of ───────────

   pants.

5. The result of their complaints ─────────── a scolding for ───────────

   poor attitude.

EXERCISE 13   Recognizing Agreement in Relative Clauses

In the following sentences, bracket the relative clauses, and underline the noun that each modifies. Underline twice the verb in each clause which agrees with this noun and draw an arrow from the verb to the noun.

EXAMPLE
Everyone [who is anyone] comes to this affair.

1. The office on the first landing above the stairs, which are to the right, is the

   place you want.

2. The husband of the two women, who were so surprised to hear themselves

   referred to as Mrs. Smith, is now in court.

3. Edna who has never experienced true love now becomes enamoured of Richard

   and George who represent themselves as fairy-tale princes.

4. Neither of these men who meet her on alternate days is the kind of man

   who intends to be faithful.

5. Her inability to decide whether George or Richard is the man who is to be

   her lover reveals the basic immaturity that is her major flaw.

EXERCISE 14   Using Verbs Within a Relative Clause

In the following sentences, bracket the relative clauses. Underline the nouns
they modify once. Supply the verbs or auxiliary verbs that agree with them.

EXAMPLE

The <u>edge</u> of the fields [which is marked by <u>evergreens</u>] [that _arrange_
themselves like soldiers on guard] runs north and south.

1. She squirted milk into the mouth of the barn cat that _____ sitting
   close to her stool.

2. Mr. Ellis, who _____ a hairy face, is eating jam tarts which _____
   smearing his moustache.

3. The practicing of our sad songs, which _____ always an effort, usually ends in laughter.

4. The butt of her jokes, which _____ rude, to put it mildly, is usually
   Conrad who _____ fortunately learned the art of ignoring them.

5. The best of her stories, which _____ all exciting, is the one about
   the mad monk who _____ really her lover in disguise.

EXERCISE 15   Using Linking Verbs That Agree with Subjects

On the lines below supply from the list of subjects one that agrees with the
verb in the sentence.

SUBJECTS: the low grades; the broken glass; cereals; bread; cars; a bus; the
treatment; the cures; the monkey's reward; the yellow bunches; lacy pink
dresses

EXAMPLE

The low grades _____ were the result of her carelessness.

1. _____ were the best food for him.

2. _____ was antibiotics and best rest.

3. _____ are always her costume.

4. _____ is their transportation.

5. _____ was the bananas.

Name _____ *Date* _____

EXERCISE 16 Reviewing Subject-Verb Agreement

In the blanks below, supply the appropriate present-tense form of the verb indicated at the left.

have 1. The committee _____ left the meeting room.

be 2. Bread with peanut butter and jelly _____ what I want for lunch.

come 3. My sister and best friend _____ by every day.

be 4. Neither my jacket nor my poles _____ here now.

be 5. Either Bud or Bill _____ to blame for the disappearance of the poles.

have 6. Those people _____ colds or the flu.

have 7. Basketball _____ me excited.

go 8. Up in the air toward the board and into the hoop _____ the ball.

jump

guard 9. I _____ high, but Sue _____ me.

be 10. The library, which _____ down the street, is where I plan to meet her.

EXERCISE 17 Reviewing Pronoun Agreement

The following paragraph is confused because the pronouns do not agree with their antecedents. Revise the paragraph to make the meaning clear. Write the revised paragraph on the lines below.

Students wishing to drop a course must get the signature of his instructors. If he won't sign, then they can appeal to the department head. If they don't agree with them, anything can happen. These can be E grades and result in withdrawal of financial aid.

_____

_____

_____

_____

_____

_____

EXERCISE 18   Correcting Agreement in Your Own Writing

Write an essay on one of the subjects listed below. Once your essay is complete, exchange it with a classmate's. Read your classmate's essay, and place a check in the margin where agreement problems exist. Now write a paragraph describing how you identified with the subject matter of your classmate's essay and what you learned from it. Attach the paragraph to the paper and return it to your classmate.

When you receive your own essay back, examine the lines opposite the check marks to see what agreement problems your classmate marked and then read the attached paragraph to find out what he or she had to say about your essay. Try using one of the subjects below:

Everybody has something to love
Something important has happened to everyone
People think a lot about their names—what they mean, where they came from, what initials they spell, and how other people view them. What thoughts do you have about your name?

8

PROBLEMS WITH MODIFIERS

Modifiers give added meaning to the nouns and verbs you use. If you understand the differences among modifiers and their systems of changes, you will use them more efficiently, eliminating the confusion between adverbs and adjectives, the misuse of comparative and superlative, and the distractions of double negatives.

Confusion of Adjectives and Adverbs   (17a)

Well and *good* are both adjectives; but *well* is also an adverb. Confusion occurs when *good* is used as an adverb in place of the adverb *well:*

> The patient is *well*. ("healthy" = adjective)
> The patient walks *well*. ("in a good manner" = adverb)
> He is a *good* patient. (adjective)

Modifiers after linking verbs should be adjectives, not adverbs:

> The smoke smells *strongly*. (adverb)
>   should be:
> The smoke smells *strong*. (adjective)

Adjectives should not be used as adverbs:

> The traffic moves *slow*.
>   should be:
> The traffic moves *slowly*.
>
> The patient walks *good*.
>   should be:
> The patient walks *well*.

Ordinal numbers are adverbs and thus do not need the *-ly* ending:

> *First*, we will go to church; *second*, we will go to dinner.

Comparative and Superlative Forms (17b)

Many adjectives and adverbs are inflected for the *comparative* degree or for the *superlative* degree. The *comparative* degree indicates more of something or a greater degree of something and uses the suffix *-er*. The superlative degree indicates the most of something or the greatest degree of something and uses the suffix *-est*.

BASE ADJECTIVE OR ADVERB	COMPARATIVE	SUPERLATIVE
bright	*brighter*	*brightest*
slow	*slower*	*slowest*
few	*fewer*	*fewest*

The comparative and superlative degrees of many adjectives and most adverbs are formed with *more* and *most* instead of the *-er* and *-est* suffixes.

slowly	*more slowly*	*most slowly*
successful	*more successful*	*most successful*

Some adjectives have irregular inflections. The most common appear below.

good	*better*	*best*
bad	*worse*	*worst*
little	*less*	*least*
some	*more*	*most*

Double Comparatives and Superlatives (17c)

Double comparatives consist of the *-er* suffix used in addition to *more*. Double comparatives should be avoided in writing and speaking.

DOUBLE COMPARATIVE	PREFERRED COMPARATIVE FORM
more better	*better*
more lovelier	*lovelier* or *more lovely*
more grander	*grander* or *more grand*

Double superlatives, which consist of the suffix *-est* in addition to the word *most*, should be avoided in writing:

Donald was the *most* noisi*est* of the ducks.
   should be:
Donald was the noisi*est* of the ducks.

Confusion of Comparative and Superlative Forms   (17d)

The comparative form is always used for comparing two things. The superlative form is used when comparing three or more things:

> Star was *bigger* than Arab.
> Star was the *biggest* of the three horses.

Modification of Absolutes   (17e)

Some adjectives and adverbs cannot be used in the comparative and superlative degrees because the meaning of the word is already superlative. Some of these words are *perfect, unique, absolute, total, excellent, supreme.*

> The diamond is *more* perfect than the ruby.
>   should be:
> The diamond is *perfect.*

Double Negatives   (17f)

Negative modifiers include *no, neither, not, never, hardly, scarcely, rarely,* and *only.* More than one negative modifier is rarely used in a single clause. The preferred form is, therefore, a single negative. Double negatives should be avoided:

> He does*n't* want *no* trouble.
>   should be:
> He does*n't* want trouble.

Exercise Objectives

Recognizing confusion between adjectives and adverbs; recognizing and using comparative and superlative forms; recognizing double superlatives and comparatives, and double negatives.

8 PROBLEMS WITH MODIFIERS _____

Name _____ *Date* _____

EXERCISE 1 Recognizing Confusion Between Adjectives and Adverbs

First, underline all adjectives in the sentences below once. Next, underline the adverbs twice; remember that adverbs often end in *-ly* and that *well* can be either an adjective or an adverb depending on its meaning. Finally, draw an arrow from the adjective to the noun it modifies and from the adverb to the verb or other adverb or adjective that it modifies.

EXAMPLE

He did well, starting with a badly rusted car and ending with a newly painted one.

1. Your dress is wrinkled badly.

2. Ian's voice sounds very weak.

3. The animal looks well.

4. The traffic flow is fast.

5. The traffic flows rapidly.

EXERCISE 2 Using Adjectives and Adverbs

Revise the following sentences using the appropriate adjective or adverb form. Write the revised sentence on the line below.

EXAMPLE
The car drives good.

The car drives well.

1. Ernestine always dresses good.

   _____

2. "How is my grandmother's health?" "She is good."

   _____

3. Lopez played fierce throughout the game.

   _____

4. The baby was screaming so loud I couldn't hear clear.

   _____

5. Alex cried pitiful because he was treated unfair.

   _____

EXERCISE 3   Using Ordinal Modifiers

In the following sentences insert an appropriate ordinal modifier. Remember the *-ly* ending is not needed.

EXAMPLE
There are four steps to assembling this stool. ___*First*___,

1. the parts must be removed from the box. _____, the stool

2. seat must be placed upside down on the floor. _____,

3. the legs should be inserted in the grooves on the underside of the seat, and _____, they must be glued in place.

4. I won't date him, _____, because he is rude, _____, because he won't comb his hair, and _____, because he hasn't asked me.

8 PROBLEMS WITH MODIFIERS _____

Name _____ *Date* _____

EXERCISE 4 Recognizing Comparative and Superlative Forms

In the following sentences, underline the comparative form once and the superlative form twice.

EXAMPLE
Jimmy wants <u>more</u> ice cream. He is the <u>greediest</u> child of all.

1. Henry wears his crown more triumphantly than before.
2. Catherine, however, continues to wear hers more graciously than he.
3. She was most doubtful of the youngest child's ability.
4. Lois' nose was blunter than Francie's.
5. Francie grew tanner and thinner as the summer progressed, and by September she was the brownest and thinnest of them all.

EXERCISE 5 Using Comparative and Superlative Forms

In the blanks below, using the base word in the margin, form a comparative in 1–5, a superlative in 6–10, and the appropriate form in 11–15.

EXAMPLES

big   My car is *bigger* than yours.

small   Mine is the *smallest* in the showroom.

high   1. My mortgage payment is _____ than yours.

quick   2. The _____ growing of the two markets is in Duluth.

little   3. She is _____ eager than he to invest.

private   4. This room is _____ than that one.

fast   5. Megan runs _____ than Myra.

high   6. The unemployment rate is _____ in my state.

private   7. I find conversations _____ in my office.

quick   8. The _____ growing of all markets is in Seattle.

little   9. She is the _____ willing among the group to invest.

fast   10. The _____ runner on the team is Isabel.

bad   11. It was the _____ looking haircut I have ever seen.

good   12. Which do you think is _____, the Ford or the Chevy?

successful **13.** Maggie managed the store _____ than Lisa.

secure   **14.** I feel _____ in my own home than here.

rapid   **15.** The Concorde flies _____ than a 747.

EXERCISE 6   Modification of Absolutes

In the sentences below, underline the preferred form of the absolute. Cross out the others.

EXAMPLE
This turtle is (the deadest / more dead / dead).

1. That sculpture is (more unique / unique).

2. Bimbo's hamburgers are (excellent / more excellent).

3. She makes the (most perfect / perfect) cake.

4. He gave his (most final / final) lecture.

5. The devastation of this city was (more total / total).

8 PROBLEMS WITH MODIFIERS

Name _____ *Date* _____

EXERCISE 7 Using Negatives Effectively

Using the negative listed in the margin, rewrite sentences 1–5 below. Rewrite
6–10 turning them into negative statements.

EXAMPLES

never   He can't tell the truth.

He never tells the truth.

Either of the cars is comfortable.

Neither of the cars is comfortable.

hardly   1. He never gives anything to anybody.

_____

not   2. I can scarcely believe it.

_____

rarely   3. She isn't in her office on Mondays.

_____

neither   4. Phil can't come either.

_____

only   5. There isn't one girl here whom I know.

_____

          6. I always take sugar in my tea.

_____

          7. It is worth the trouble.

_____

          8. So you have a hammer?

_____

          9. We have fifty cents between us.

_____

          10. I'll tell on you!

_____

EXERCISE 8   Recognizing Preferred Forms of Modifiers: Review

In the following sentences, underline the preferred form.

1. I will wait a (little more longer / little longer).

2. That book is (the most excellent / excellent).

3. Gigi styles hair (beautiful / beautifully).

4. Go (quick / quickly).

5. Model 200 is (the best of / the better of) the three.

6. This poem is (more unique than the other / unique).

7. I haven't got (no books / any books).

8. Which of the two do you like (better / best)?

9. He hasn't (scarcely a chance / a chance).

10. She will (sure / surely) win.

EXERCISE 9   Finding Adjectives and Adverbs in Your Own Writing

A judge in Ohio orders people who have been convicted of driving while drunk to attend the autopsies of victims of traffic accidents. Is his sentence too hard or too easy? Can you think of a more appropriate one?

Write a short essay in which you answer these questions. Consider that your essay is a contribution to a class discussion of the problem of people who drive while drunk. Perhaps you can exchange papers or start a verbal discussion with your classmates.

In your essay underline the adjectives and adverbs once. Underline again each one that is comparative or superlative.

9

CRAFTING SENTENCES

Successful sentence crafting depends in part upon your skill in placing ideas into words, phrases, and clauses in ways that make their relationships clear and their relative importance apparent. Practice in coordinating and embedding clauses and phrases, in constructing different kinds of sentences, and in using repetition and word order to achieve emphasis will help you become skilled in composing effective sentences.

Coordination   (18a)

Sentences can be combined by using coordinating conjunctions such as *and, for, or, but, nor, so,* and *yet.*

> The pillows were aired. The blankets were washed. The sheets were washed.
>> can become:
>
> The pillows were aired *and* the blankets *and* sheets were washed.

Sentences can also be combined by using correlative conjunctions such as *both / and, either / or, neither / nor, not only / but also,* and conjunctive adverbs such as *also(,), besides(,), finally(,), however(,), then(,).*

Embedding   (18b)

Embedding of Adverbial Clauses

Sentences can be combined by changing one or more into a subordinate clause:

> He goes. She goes.
>> can become:
>
> ADVERBIAL CLAUSE   ADVERBIAL CLAUSE
> [Where he goes], she goes.   (or)   [Because he goes], she goes.

Embedding of Relative Clauses

Sentences can be combined by changing one sentence into a relative clause and embedding it in the other:

> Jim Donaldson was back at work Wednesday. He had suffered a rib injury. The rib injury required him to wear a flak vest.
>> can become:

RELATIVE CLAUSE   RELATIVE CLAUSE

Jim Donaldson [who suffered a rib injury] [which required him to wear a flak vest] was back at work Wednesday.

Embedding of Participial Phrases

Sentences can be combined by changing one or more sentences into participial phrases and embedding them in another:

The chief inspector walked around. He hummed to himself. He was reminiscent of a big bumble bee.
can become:

PARTICIPIAL PHRASES

[Walking about] and [humming to himself], the chief inspector was reminiscent of a big bumble bee.

Embedding of Single Words and Prepositional Phrases

Sentences can be combined by changing one or more sentences into adjectives or prepositional phrases and embedding them in another:

The car was a new model. It was a racing car. It had long lines. The lines gleamed.
can become:
The new model racing car had long gleaming lines.

Embedding of Absolutes

Sentences can be combined by changing one or more into absolutes:

The old crocodile nodded confidently. Our family sat as still as a stone.
can become:

ABSOLUTE PHRASE

[The old crocodile nodding confidently], our family sat as still as a stone.

Cumulative Sentences and Free Modifiers   (18c)

A cumulative sentence begins with a base clause that contains the main assertion of the sentence. The base clause is followed by modifiers that refer back to it (or to a preceding phrase or clause) and that add information about it as the sentence progresses. The modifiers can be adjectives, adverbs, participial phrases, subordinate and relative clauses, absolutes, and appositives:

BASE CLAUSE   PARTICIPIAL PHRASE

The white mare was alone on a green field, [galloping back and forth

PARTICIPIAL PHRASE

with her head and tail high], [bouncing stiff-legged to a halt at the fence],

PARTICIPIAL PHRASE   ADVERBIAL CLAUSE

[snorting loudly], [before she would wheel in the opposite direction].

Periodic Sentences   (18d)

The main clause of a periodic sentence occurs just before the period and following the modifiers. The modifiers, which can be phrases or clauses, move the readers toward the subject, shaping the impression of it before it is encountered:

PREPOSITIONAL PHRASES
[Past the wall of piled stones carved in script with Buddhist prayers], [past

PREPOSITIONAL PHRASE
a deserted village, terraced fields lying untended and stunted pine trees],

PARTICIPIAL PHRASE   BASE CLAUSE
[always skirting the slopes of the mountain], *we wandered the day away.*

Repetition of Words, Patterns, and Sounds   (18e)

The repetition of important words, structural patterns, or sounds in a sentence or among sentences will help emphasize certain ideas:

Over the first hill, *over* the second and *on* and *on,* there was nothing but *trees, trees, trees.*

In addition, repeated patterns containing similar or contrasting ideas give emphasis to the similarities and differences between the ideas:

He *hoped* for the *best* but *prepared* for the *worst.*
He *told* me and I *told* you: then, we both *told* Mrs. Holmes.

Variations in Word Order   (18g)

You can cause slight changes in the meaning and rhetorical effect of what you are writing by varying sentence structures and moving sentence parts. There are three rules to remember when you vary word order:

• Most emphasis occurs at the end of a sentence.
• Second most emphasis occurs at the beginning of a sentence.
• Least emphasis occurs in the middle of the sentence.

In addition, a complement position is stronger than a middle position.

Shifting from Passive to Active or the Reverse

The transformation of a sentence in the active voice into one in the passive takes the emphasis from the original subject and places it on the original direct or indirect object.

S   IO   DO
ACTIVE: *Randy* showed *Joan* the *car.*
S   DO   IO
PASSIVE: *Joan* was shown the *car* by *Randy.*

Transforming the passive voice to the active will have the effect of placing the doer of the action in the subject position as you can see by the example of the active voice sentence above.

It is also possible to deemphasize the doer of the action in a passive sentence by dropping the *by* phrase:

The *car* was shown to Joan; or *Joan* was shown the *car*.

It and *There* Patterns

Sentences can be converted so that *it* or *there* acts as a place holder for the subject. The effect is to move the original subject into a complement position and, thus, give it added emphasis.

Alain wins the race every time.
It is *Alain* who wins the race every time.
Four bands played last Friday.
There were *four bands* playing last Friday.

Moving Sentence Parts

An emphasis can be changed by shifting a part of a sentence to a position where it will receive more or less emphasis depending on what is desired. In addition, remember that any unusual inversion will place emphasis on the elements not in their normal position.

She spoils my <u>dreams</u> by showing me the real world.
    can become:
By showing me the real world, she always spoils my <u>dreams</u>.

They played <u>off-key</u> without knowing it.
    can become:
They played, without knowing it, <u>off-key</u>.

Emphasis can also be created by interrupting the normal forward movement of a sentence:

Nights, <u>especially Saturday nights</u>, she sat in the dark listening to the heels clicking on the sidewalk.

Exercise Objectives

Practice in making new sentences through coordination, embedding, and using free modifiers; composing cumulative and periodic sentences; using repetition of words, patterns, and sounds to focus on meaning; changing word order to achieve emphasis.

9 CRAFTING SENTENCES

Name _____ Date _____

EXERCISE 1   Combining Sentences Through Coordination

Using one of the coordinating conjunctions combine the following sentence groups. Write the combined sentence on the line below.

EXAMPLE
The left hemisphere of the brain controls the right side of the body.
The right hemisphere controls the left side of the body.
The left side alone controls speech.

The left hemisphere of the brain controls the right side of the body and the right hemisphere controls the left side, yet the left side alone controls speech.

1. Dogs need to be fed once a day.
   They should not be given milk.
   Dogs should not be fed chicken bones.

   _____

   _____

   _____

2. When you talk to someone, you receive immediate feedback.
   When you write to someone, you must understand what your reader needs to know.
   You must understand what will interest him or her.

   _____

   _____

   _____

3. I got caught in traffic.
   I couldn't find a parking spot.
   I made it to class on time.

   _____

   _____

   _____

4. He maintains an impeccable appearance.
   He neglects his personal finances.
   He is a workaholic.

   _____

   _____

   _____

5. Mrs. Holmes admires Indian rugs.
   She would love to own one.
   She has never tried to purchase one.

_____

_____

_____

EXERCISE 2   Combining Sentences Using Correlative Conjunctions or Conjunctive Adverbs

Using appropriate correlative conjunctions or conjunctive adverbs combine the following sentence groups. Write the new sentence on the lines below.

EXAMPLES

They opened out onto the patio for light. They were used for ventilation.

They opened out onto the patio not only for light but also for ventilation.

The city was constructed on a geometrical pattern. Within it, huge avenues crossed each other at right angles.

The city was constructed on a geometrical pattern; therefore, within it, huge avenues crossed each other at right angles

1. Photosynthesis is an exclusive function of plants.
   Respiration is common to both plants and animals.

_____

_____

2. A maimed hydra can quickly replace a lost part. A maimed part cannot

   replace a lost hydra. _____

_____

3. The dictionary was no help. The thesaurus wasn't either.

_____

_____

4. All life on earth feeds on radiation coming from a middle-aged star called

   the sun. Life is a product of starlight.

_____

_____

Name _____ *Date* _____

EXERCISE 3   Combining Sentences by Embedding Adverbial Clauses

Combine the following sentences by turning one into an adverbial clause and embedding it in the other. Write the new sentence on the line below and bracket the adverbial clause.

EXAMPLE
The weather station forecast frost for tonight.
The orange growers will start their smudge pots.

The orange growers will start their smudge pots [because the weather station forecast frost for tonight].

1. Jonathan demanded we start.
   He was three-quarters of an hour early.

   _____

   _____

2. Dad had gone hunting.
   The baby was born.

   _____

   _____

3. I saw Mrs. Phillips in the store.
   I remembered owing her the sugar.

   _____

   _____

4. We saw dirty dishes, dusty floors, and a greasy stove.
   We decided Arthur needed our help.

   _____

   _____

5. He had a second cup of coffee.
   We waited by the Spanish steps.

   _____

   _____

EXERCISE 4   Combining Sentences by Embedding Relative Clauses

Combine the following sentences by turning one into a relative clause and embedding it in the other. Write the new sentence on the line below and bracket the relative clause.

EXAMPLE
The woman was correct in her identification.
The woman saw the murderer on the train.

The woman, [who saw the murderer on the train], was correct in her identification.

1. The farmer's daughter set out the food.
   The daughter was marrying the milkman.

   _____

   _____

2. The huge roast of beef sat on the platter.
   The beef was marbled with fat.

   _____

   _____

3. People dress to show that they belong to a special group.
   These people range from rock singers to executives.

   _____

   _____

4. Dick placed his guns on the mantelpiece.
   We trusted Dick.

   _____

   _____

5. I bought my study guide for biology at the university bookstore. My study guide cost as much as the textbook.

   _____

   _____

Name _____ *Date* _____

EXERCISE 5   Combining Sentences by Embedding Participial Phrases

Combine the following sentences by turning all but one into participial phrases and embedding them in the remaining sentence. Write the new sentence on the line below and bracket each participial phrase.

EXAMPLE

Josie Beard overflowed with talent.
She played the cello.
She won at Monopoly.
She made brownies.

[Playing the cello], [winning at Monopoly], [making brownies], Josie Beard overflowed with talent.

1. The women walk their dogs.
   The women carry their children.
   The women make their way to the park.

   _____

   _____

2. "I am not the maid!" she used to shout.
   She would storm through my room.
   She would pick up skirts and jeans.
   She would hang them in the closet.

   _____

   _____

3. The Canadian coast guard began a search.
   They had received the message that lifeboats had been sighted in the Gulf of
   St. Lawrence.

   _____

   _____

   _____

4. The townspeople protected the beached whale from the sun until the tide came in.
They poured water over it.
They covered it with a tarpaulin.

_____

_____

_____

5. He gripped my wrist.
He pulled steadily.
He got me out of the quicksand.

_____

_____

_____

EXERCISE 6 Combining Sentences by Embedding Adjectives and Prepositional Phrases

Combine the following sentences by turning two or three of them into adjectives or prepositional phrases and embedding these in the remaining one. Write the new sentence on the line below and bracket newly embedded adjectives or prepositional phrases.

EXAMPLE
The river has muddy banks.
The trees overhang the banks.
The water irises are pale blue.
These flowers cling to the roots of the trees.

Trees [with [pale blue] water irises] [clinging to their roots] overhang the [muddy] banks [of the river].

1. The whistle sounds.
The sound is strident.
The workers are sent streaming out of the factory.
The factory makes tires.

_____

_____

_____

2. Jobs were created.
The jobs were new.
A factory opened creating the jobs.

_____

_____

_____

3. McEwen's chimney is giving off little puffs.
The puffs are smoke and are rising.
The sky is blue.

_____

_____

_____

4. How did the man drown wading across a creek?
The man was six feet tall.
The creek had an average depth of six inches.

_____

_____

_____

5. The name of the symphony is the Boston Symphony.
The symphony is famous.
Many Americans have heard it perform.
Television and radio have broadcast the performances.

_____

_____

_____

EXERCISE 7   Combining Sentences by Using Absolutes

Combine the following sentences by turning one or two into absolutes and joining them with another. Write the new sentence on the line below.

EXAMPLE
He and his brother knelt on the dry, red beech leaves.
Their faces were pressed against their hands.
The tree trunks were rising sharply above.

_Their faces pressed against their hands,
he and his brother knelt on the dry, red beech
leaves, tree trunks rising sharply above them._

1. Sir Ghastly Graves lived in a coffin.
His only night out was Halloween.

_____

_____

2. I can't get my sleep.
My husband snores.
The mattress is lumpy.
The trees make strange tapping sounds against the window.

_____

_____

_____

3. Ninety percent of Americans do not understand the facts of life.
Men believe that women have all the answers.
Women believe that men have all the answers.

_____

_____

_____

4. Paula watched the car wind up the road toward the airport.
The tears streamed down her face.

_____

_____

_____

5. My friends drop by.
The telephone rings.
The doorbell rings.
I can't finish my homework.

_____

_____

_____

_____

Name ─────────────────────────── *Date* ──────────

EXERCISE 8   Recognizing Cumulative Sentences I

In the following sentences underline the base clause. Bracket each of the phrases and clauses that refers back to the base clause or to a preceding phrase or clause.

EXAMPLE

Every morning she tried to touch her fingers to her toes, [forcing her knees painfully backward] and [groaning while she stretched to make contact].

1. The singers were still singing, drowning out the guitarists who were trying to play an accompaniment to the ragged song.

2. She looked so confused, standing there on the grass with her oversized rake and with her mouth trembling while the wind scattered her neat piles of leaves.

3. He would sit at the little table, talking horse racing, basketball, and politics, telling anecdotes of the movie stars, giving information on the best restaurants, and reporting the finest places for Americans to stay in Europe.

4. He poured the bottle of ink into the mousehole, perhaps coloring the gray mouse black but certainly surprising it with a flood of liquid that it would carry on its paws while marking the linoleum with tiny footprints.

5. The old servant hurried to obey, pulling aside the curtain, sliding glass panels open which let the cool fresh air drift across the room.

EXERCISE 9 Recognizing Cumulative Sentences II

In the following cumulative sentences underline the base clause. Bracket each adjective, adverb, appositive, and absolute that refers back to it or to a preceding phrase or clause.

EXAMPLE

It was an emergency sound, [an ambulance wail], [bold and eerie].

1. We roasted chestnuts in midday August, sweat pouring down our faces, and our backs turning the color of the burnt nutshells.

2. Spot loved her, expectantly, joyously, and unreservedly.

3. Who was that woman, the lady with the arrogant step, the princess with the cold blue eyes, haughty and unsmiling?

4. The sparrow was captive in the bag of bird seed, his wings beating frantically toward freedom in the midst of a tremendous feast.

5. My favorite class is English literature, a hard subject to some but easy for me.

EXERCISE 10 Constructing Cumulative Sentences I

Using the base clauses below, construct cumulative sentences. Use your imagination to develop the phrases and clauses for the sentences.

EXAMPLE
Imagine that you have just won the lottery.

I was hysterical 1. _hugging the telephone and the dog,_
            2. _crying and laughing, and_
            3. _yelling to the neighborhood,_
            "I am a millionaire!"

1. *Imagine that you have been caught in a rainstorm.*

   The downpour came suddenly 1. _____
                       2. _____
                       3. _____

2. Imagine that you are the solitary canoeist on a quiet lake.

I pushed the canoe into the water **1.** _____

　　　　　　　　　　　　　　　　2. _____

　　　　　　　　　　　　　　　　3. _____

3. Imagine that you have been captured by an alien spacecraft.

Something grabbed me **1.** _____

　　　　　　　　　　　　2. _____

　　　　　　　　　　　　3. _____

4. Imagine that you are rescuing people from a burning building.

I rushed in **1.** _____

　　　　　　2. _____

　　　　　　3. _____

5. Imagine that you have your favorite meal before you.

I tucked my napkin under my chin **1.** _____

　　　　　　　　　　　　　　　　2. _____

　　　　　　　　　　　　　　　　3. _____

EXERCISE 11　Constructing Cumulative Sentences II

Combine the following sentences so as to make cumulative sentences. Change the structure of all but the base sentence into clauses, phrases, adjectives, appositives, or absolutes.

EXAMPLE
The smock was silk.
It was brightly colored with an orange print.
She changed into a smock after her excursion on the bus.
The bus was covered with grime and smelled of exhaust.

She changed into a smock, silk and brightly colored with an orange print, after her excursion on the bus that was covered with grime and smelled of exhaust.

1. We climbed up onto the glacier.
   The light of the dawn softened the profile of the mountain.
   We carefully kicked steps in the ice.

   _____

   _____

   _____

2. I wish you could see what I saw there.
   It was on that first morning.
   It was through a veil of lightly falling rain.
   It was a little city made of adobe built into the rock face.

   _____

   _____

   _____

3. It is an epoch of geologic calm.
   Warm shallow waters spread over the land.
   Coral and marine organisms live and die.
   Their skeletons drift to the floor.

   _____

   _____

   _____

4. Jobs are available here.
   Merchandise passes through this port.
   Money is invested here.
   These activities produce an economic future.
   The future is continuously promising.

   _____

   _____

   _____

   _____

5. Crazy Horse and his people made their way.
   They went through the sleet.
   Their goal was the familiar country of Little Powder.
   Their friends were there.
   These friends were hidden from the elements in elfskin tents.
   These friends had a hidden supply of food.

   _____

   _____

   _____

   _____

   _____

Name _____ *Date* _____

EXERCISE 12   Recognizing Periodic Sentences

In the following sentences, bracket each of the phrases or clauses preceding the base clause and underline the base clause.

EXAMPLE

Now, [after reaching that coveted twenty-win two years running], [after rising to national prominence as the ace of the staff], [after surviving a rocky first game start], <u>Craig has earned the right to gloat.</u>

1. According to Dr. Jock, according to my mother, but not according to my father, I jog too much.

2. Despite his job record, despite his marital status, and only because he is nineteen, his car insurance is high.

3. If you don't read advertisements carefully, if you don't order merchandise carefully, and, above all, if you don't check out the company, you may lose money buying by mail.

4. My brothers having divorced their wives, my sisters having separated from their husbands, I am the only child with an old-fashioned, traditional marriage.

5. Staring through the window at the dusk, bumping our heels with a slow rhythm against our chairs, we waited.

EXERCISE 13   Constructing Periodic Sentences

In the following sentence groups, combine the first sentences with the others to make a periodic sentence.

EXAMPLE
Snow was turning to hail.
The streets were turning to ice.
My brakes were sticking.
I finally made it here.

Even though the snow was turning to hail, The streets were turning to ice, and my brakes were sticking, I finally made it here.

1. It carries a maximum fine of $125,000.
   It carries a possible jail term of up to fifteen years.
   It carries a double maximum for a second offense.
   A conviction for drug trafficking is serious.

_____

_____

_____

_____

2. His chin was between his thumb and his forefinger.
   Only his twitching nose revealed his feelings.
   He sat hungry and impatient.

_____

_____

_____

3. Tea is a drink which warms and invigorates.
   Tea is a drink fit for kings and queens.
   A cup of tea is what I need.

_____

_____

_____

4. I traveled thirteen hours by air.
   Then I journeyed five hours by train.
   Last I walked six miles.
   I arrived in the little village in India.

_____

_____

_____

_____

5. He is honored by all he works with.
   He is loved by all his students.
   He is remembered for his prolific scholarship.
   Professor Jones accepts retirement.

_____

_____

_____

_____

Name _____ *Date* _____

EXERCISE 14 Recognizing and Using Words Repeated for Rhetorical Effect

In *a*, underline the words repeated for emphasis. In *b*, write a paragraph in which you repeat a significant word for emphasis.

a. I knew somehow that I could conform to all the rules and be a model student. And I did. Every morning I'd arrive at school on time and would stand erect in the boys' line waiting for the front door to the massive, red-brick building to open. Once inside the school, the ritual of lines continued. We lined up to use the lavatory, and we lined up at the end of the day to go home. I can remember one particular day when the 3:30 P.M. bell rang, and we lined up outside our homeroom, waiting in the vast, spacious hall for the signal to retrieve our wraps from our locker.

b. You might describe someone who is very old, happy, or angry; you might write out something you learned from a lecture given in a course and repeat important words for emphasis; or you might write a note to someone reporting on an event you attended and repeat significant words. *Reminder:* repetition of *un*important words places emphasis on *un*important ideas.

EXERCISE 15 Recognizing and Using Repeated Patterns

In the sentences given below, bracket the patterns that are repeated. Then compose sentences containing repeated patterns similar in form to those in the sentence models.

EXAMPLE
[She stands] [inside the door], or [she stands] [outside the gate], or [at the corner], always waiting.

The sand hides between my toes, or it hides in my socks, or in my bed.

1. *Gerund Subject repeated:*
   Cycling in England, hiking in Germany, and swimming in the Adriatic are my ambitions.

   _____

   _____

   _____

2. *Participial Phrase repeated:*
Meddling in my business, prying in my love affairs, ordering me about, Uncle Cleveland is a lovable nuisance.

_____

_____

_____

3. *Infinitive Subject repeated:*
To leave the office, to step into my car, to drive home, and then to smell beef stew as I open the door is heaven.

_____

_____

_____

4. *Adverbial Clause repeated:*
I love her even though she loses her temper, even though she comes home late, forgets birthdays, breaks promises, and drops wet towels on the floor.

_____

_____

_____

5. *Balanced Pattern*
In a job search a negative attitude breeds failure; a positive attitude, success.

_____

_____

_____

9 CRAFTING SENTENCES

Name _____ *Date* _____

EXERCISE 16   Changing Active and Passive Sentences

Change the sentences that are in the active voice to the passive so that the emphasis falls upon the original direct object or indirect object. Change the sentences that are in the passive voice to the active making the emphasis fall upon the original direct or indirect object.

EXAMPLE
Active to passive: Joseph painted the shed bright red.

The shed was painted bright red by Joseph.

Passive to active: Our cat had been frightened by the raccoon on the roof.

The raccoon on the roof had frightened our cat.

1. The station was kept open by Dave, who did everything from pumping gas to installing mufflers.

_____

_____

2. Leon hit the ball straight down the fairway.

_____

_____

_____

3. A blue balloon had been swallowed by Duffy at his master's birthday party.

_____

_____

_____

4. Chemical companies produce new insecticides each year which have the potential for damaging plant and animal life.

_____

_____

_____

5. A select audience was shown the new models by the person who had designed them.

_____

_____

_____

EXERCISE 17   Using the *It* and *There* Patterns.

Revise the following sentence to the *it* or *there* pattern, writing the revised sentences on the lines below. Underline the words in the subject complement position now receiving a new emphasis.

EXAMPLE
High temperatures ruined the corn crop.

It was high temperatures that ruined the corn crop.

1. The city is beautiful, indeed.

_____

2. To dream of applause is easy.

_____

3. A flock of sparrows is swaying on the wire.

_____

4. I remember the sound of rifle fire from the last guerilla attack.

_____

_____

5. An incredible amount of confusion exists. Outside, someone is knocking to get in; inside, someone is crying to get out.

_____

_____

Name ―――――――――――――――――――― *Date* ――――――――

EXERCISE 18 Changing the Position of Parts of a Sentence

In the following sentences, change the position of sentence parts so that the underlined part receives a greater emphasis. Write the revised sentence on the line following.

EXAMPLE

Joan smiled after complaining for a full week.   *After complaining for a full week, Joan smiled.*

1. He agreed to the <u>plan</u> except for one feature. ――――――――

――――――――――――――――――――――――――――――

2. The author, <u>literate</u> and <u>well-informed</u>, traces the course <u>of artificial intelligence</u> from its mythic beginnings to its possibilities in the future. ――――――

――――――――――――――――――――――――――――――

――――――――――――――――――――――――――――――

――――――――――――――――――――――――――――――

3. Colin gazed <u>at her</u> adoringly. ――――――――――――――

――――――――――――――――――――――――――――――

4. There are <u>six puppies</u>, snuggling down or bounding about the kitchen.

――――――――――――――――――――――――――――――

――――――――――――――――――――――――――――――

5. I love first and foremost the <u>burnished gleam</u> of her hair. ――――――――

――――――――――――――――――――――――――――――

――――――――――――――――――――――――――――――

EXERCISE 19 Finding the Proper Emphasis in Your Own Writing

Write an essay informing an interested older person of your response to the following subjects:

Coed dorms inevitably lead to more sexual involvement

Young men today are still more attracted to shy, passive women than to assertive, confident women

Big families foster security (rivalry)

An only child has advantages (disadvantages).

Once you have produced a rough draft, experiment with sentence structure and word order so as to emphasize your most important points.

10

REVISING SENTENCES

You may compose carefully in order to establish relationships among ideas and to achieve emphasis but still discover in your rough draft that some of the sentences are not totally clear. If this is the case, it will help to know what problems cause confusion in sentences and how to eliminate them.

Problems in Coordination   (19a)

Sometimes sentences are written in a coordinate structure when their parts are not really coordinate. Sentences should be revised to show the logical relationships within the sentence:

> My older brother cried, and we were young, and didn't understand, and we were scared.
>
> can be revised as:
>
> *When* my older brother cried, we were scared *because* we were young and didn't understand what was wrong.

Problems in Subordination   (19b)

Sometimes subordinate structures are not clear either because their content is not logically subordinate to the base clause or because an inappropriate subordinating conjunction is used.

> *When* the usual newscast is only a half-hour in length, newscasters have difficulty in communicating the details of the news.
>
> can be revised as:
>
> *Because* the usual newscast is only a half-hour in length, newscasters have difficulty in communicating the details of the news.

Problems in Modification   (19c)

Split Infinitives

Sometimes modifiers are placed so that they create confusion. If modifiers split an infinitive, the meaning of the sentence may not be clear.

I want *to* really *discover* what happened.
    can be revised as:
I want *to discover* what really happened.
    or:
I really want *to discover* what happened.

Placement of Prepositions

Sometimes a preposition placed at the end of a sentence causes the natural stress at the end of the sentence to be weakened:

He doesn't know the address he lives *at*.
    can be revised as:
He doesn't know the address *at* which he lives.
    or
He doesn't know his address.

Placement of Phrases and Clauses

Phrases and clauses should be placed where it will be evident what they modify:

The jackets in this store *for sale* are very cheap.
    can be revised as:
The jackets *for sale* in this store are very cheap.

Dangling Modifiers

Dangling modifiers are modifiers with nothing to modify. Participial, prepositional, gerund, and infinitive phrases and elliptical clauses sometimes appear in dangling forms:

Perspiring profusely, the vacuuming was finished.
    can be revised as:
The housekeeper *perspired profusely* after finishing the vacuuming.

Problems with Passives (19d)

The passive voice can effectively produce certain emphases in meaning, but it sometimes becomes tedious and difficult to understand. It is wise, therefore, to be cautious in using the passive voice:

PASSIVE VOICE: Steve *was considered* by Elsie for a transfer because he *was felt* by his colleagues in the office to be dishonest. His annoying presence in the office *could be eliminated* if he *were transferred*.
    can become:
ACTIVE VOICE: Elsie *considered* Steve for a transfer because his office colleagues felt him to be dishonest. Elsie *could eliminate* his annoying presence from the office if she *transferred* him.

Problems with Predication   (19f)

Problems with predication arise when there is a mismatch between the subject and its predicate or between elements within the predicate.

Mismatches occur when the predicate requires a predicate noun or adjective following a linking verb, but it contains instead an adverbial clause:

ADVERBIAL CLAUSE
The loss is *because they batted poorly.*
   should be:

NOUN
The loss is the *result* of their batting poorly.
   or:

They lost because they batted poorly.

Mismatches occur when the verb requires a noun object (usually in the form of a noun clause) but an adverbial clause is used in its place:

I heard *where classes were cancelled.*
   should become:
I heard *that classes were cancelled.*

Mismatches occur when the subject and predicate do not relate to each other logically.

My mother's copper-bottomed pans are shinier *than Aunt Jane.*
   should be:
My mother's copper-bottomed pans are shinier *than Aunt Jane's* (pans).

Problems with Parallel Structure   (19g)

Three problems with parallelism occur frequently: the obscuring of parallel ideas by not expressing them in parallel fashion; the joining of unequal parts with a coordinating conjunction; and the confusing of parallel ideas by the misplacement of correlative conjunctions.

Obscuring Parallel Ideas

A problem in clarity or emphasis occurs when the ideas meant to be parallel are not expressed in parallel fashion:

The handling of each child might be different. She might treat the six-year-old for coughing with cough medicine while the infant wouldn't be given the same medicine but probably an antihistamine.
   could become:
She might handle each child's cough differently, *treating the six-year-old with cough medicine* and *the infant with an antihistamine.*

Coordinating Structures of Unequal Function

Problems in clarity and emphasis occur when the parallelism is lacking in a place where it should occur. The two clauses or phrases on each side of a coordinating conjunction should be equal in function:

> They can cause different diseases and *in content of chemicals.*
>   could become:
> They can cause different diseases and *contain different chemicals.*

Confusing Parallel Structures

Problems in clarity arise when correlative conjunctions are placed so as to confuse parallel ideas. In an effective sentence, the elements following each part of a correlative conjunction are equivalent:

> The team must *either* win *or* it must retire.
>   should become:
> *Either* the team must win *or* it must retire.
>   or:
> The team *either* must win *or* must retire.

Exercise Objectives

Revising problems in coordination and subordination; revising misplaced pepositional phrases, clauses, and modifiers; revising dangling phrases; revising problems with passives, predication, and parallel structure.

Name _____ *Date* _____

EXERCISE 1 Revising Confused Coordination

Revise the following unclear coordinate constructions. Write the revised sentence on the lines below.

EXAMPLE
We were the fifth group on, and we figured we would go backstage to rehearse a little.

Because we were the fifth group on, we figured we had time to go backstage to rehearse a little.

1. The other performers started to crowd around, and we stopped playing.

   _____

   _____

2. I got within a block of home, and I turned on all the speed I had, and I ran so fast, and my gym shoes had blow-outs, and all you could see were my elbows and the seat of my pants.

   _____

   _____

   _____

   _____

3. His church was sponsoring a talent show, and he wanted his group to perform, and we all agreed.

   _____

   _____

4. My career goal is to become a nurse and there are jobs in nursing.

   _____

   _____

5. The first historian was Herodotus and he was a Greek and he probably wrote between 484 and 425 B.C.

   _____

   _____

EXERCISE 2 Revising Confused Subordination

In the following sentences, the subordinate clause is not logically related to the base clause. Underline the subordinate clause. Revise the sentence to achieve clarity, and write the revised sentence on the line below.

EXAMPLE

This was my first time trying out for a team while I didn't know anyone.

This was the first time I tried out for a team on which I didn't know anyone.

1. Myra was frightened because she doggedly hung on to me.

_____

_____

2. The relatives stay too long, while my mother gets tired.

_____

3. As I landed in shock, I came down.

_____

4. When the ball came flying out to half court was when I glided up to the basket where I slammed the ball on the back of the basket.

_____

_____

5. When all those trips back to the South began, my family migrated from the South.

_____

_____

6. While Pat wanted to make a home run, she knew that she couldn't.

_____

7. Where there were quite a few embarrassing moments, I think the most humiliating one had to do with an ice cream cone.

_____

_____

8. She continued to talk when I retaliated by saying that I didn't care when it wasn't her business.

_____

_____

9. I never expected to lose anything I owned where I considered myself impregnable.

_____

_____

10. There is a new book by Marge Piercy where the changes of two women are described.

_____

_____

EXERCISE 3   Revising Split Infinitives

In the following sentences, underline the two parts of the infinitive. Bracket the modifier that splits it. Revise the sentence and write the new sentence on the line below.

EXAMPLE
My task is to [quickly but fairly] fire the malingerers.

My task is to fire the malingerers quickly but fairly.

1. To never go back would be too sad.

_____

2. He failed to completely comprehend.

_____

3. I don't want you to without caring for my comfort throw your belongings around the room.

_____

_____

4. Princetta wanted to not get even but to win.

_____

5. Alex tries to basically strangle the guitar.

_____

EXERCISE 4   Moving Phrases and Clauses for Clarity

In the following sentences, phrases and clauses are misplaced. Underline the phrase or clause that is misplaced. Revise the sentence to make the meaning clear, and write the revised sentence on the line below.

EXAMPLE

Getting up so early was difficult for Matthew <u>to go to school</u>.

Getting up so early to go to school was difficult for matthew.

1. The line was busy because I knew she was talking to Craig, and I raged.

_____

_____

2. Don't go alone, Peter, although Sue can't go with you because you won't have as much fun.

_____

_____

3. Cost-effective advertising must bring a large number of customers in the clothing trade.

_____

_____

4. The woman at the loom looked like an old etching weaving her rug.

_____

_____

5. At the intersection of Trumbull and Warren, the mechanic from that garage fixed the muffler.

_____

_____

Name _____ *Date* _____

EXERCISE 5 Revising Dangling Modifiers I

The following sentences contain dangling prepositional, infinitive, and gerund phrases. Underline the dangling phrase and revise the sentence to correct ambiguity. Write the revised sentence on the lines below.

EXAMPLE
Before calling the police, the burglars got away.

Before I called the police, The burglars got away.

1. After declaring a knockout, the fight stopped.

_____

_____

2. Children must be hospitalized when machines and medication aren't available at home, such as leukemia.

_____

_____

3. In using the telephone, the voice must be clear and crisp.

_____

_____

4. Before appearing on the program, the dance recital had lasted two hours.

_____

_____

5. To eat slowly, it is best to eat less that way.

_____

_____

6. Unable to avoid a speeding fine, the judge ignored my plea.

_____

_____

7. To love your neighbor, it is a happier life if you live like this.

_____

_____

8. Because of waiting so long, boredom resulted.

_____

_____

9. Before examining the budget, the money disappeared.

_____

_____

10. Able to reach the top of the shelf, the dishes were put away quickly by Marcia.

_____

_____

EXERCISE 6   Revising Dangling Modifiers II

The following sentences contain dangling elliptical phrases. Underline the dangling phrase. Revise the sentence to correct ambiguity, and write the revised sentence on the line below.

EXAMPLE
 <u>Although a huge load</u>, the truck managed the haul.

Although its load was huge, the truck managed the haul.

1. When finally out of sight, he still heard the plane.

_____

2. When faced with failure, the depression set in.

_____

3. Once finished, the pleasure over his degree was obvious.

_____

4. Although aware of the cost, the set was purchased.

_____

5. They fired him after working for twenty-eight years.

_____

EXERCISE 7   Revising Dangling Modifiers III

The following sentences contain dangling participial phrases. Underline the phrase. Revise the sentence to correct the confusion, and write the revised sentence on the line below.

EXAMPLE
Making his subordinates work long hours, I dreaded working for Louie.

I dreaded working for Louie because he made his subordinates work long hours.

1. Eating celery, radishes, and greens, the extra weight disappeared.

_____

_____

2. Running after the ice-cream truck, the driver was stopped.

_____

_____

3. Knitting rapidly, my sister's sweater grew.

_____

_____

4. Filling quickly, the judge closed the courtroom door.

_____

5. Running the stop sign, it seems remarkable to me that cars have had no accidents at the four-way stop street.

_____

_____

EXERCISE 8   Revising Misplaced, Squinting, and Dangling Modifiers

In the following sentences, underline the misplaced, squinting, or dangling modifier. Revise the sentence and write it on the line below.

EXAMPLE
Bored by television, playing cards became our entertainment.

Because we were bored by television, we entertained ourselves by playing cards.

1. A limited number of cars are available at substantial savings that are unclaimed or damaged.

_____

_____

2. Suffering excruciating pain, the accident has resulted in a back injury.

_____

_____

3. He pushes him aside feeling his betrayal.

_____

4. Hotels should reserve their lower floors for smokers only, placing non-smokers on the upper floors, where they can't be trapped by fire.

_____

_____

5. The index is sectioned off by subjects, which is turned out yearly.

_____

_____

6. Palmer only is paying attention to Donna.

_____

7. You can hike to fish the fifteen miles of river into the Beauchamp area.

_____

_____

8. While licking its fur, Sir James spotted the fox.

_____

9. The supervisor thought today I should go home.

_____

10. The interurban coach stalled on the expressway, which was filled with homebound passengers.

_____

_____

Name _____   *Date* _____

EXERCISE 9   Recognizing and Revising the Passive Voice

In the following sentences, underline the passive voice verbs. Write the revised sentence in active voice on the lines below, and underline the active voice verbs.

EXAMPLE

The part of the problem that <u>was found</u> to be the most difficult <u>was identified</u> as the first step.

The first step of the problem <u>was</u> the most difficult part.

1. The evidence against him was admitted by Evan to be damning. He was discovered by Paul with the vault open and his hand on the money.

   _____

   _____

   _____

2. Her anxiety was increased by the presence of Mr. Conniff.

   _____

3. The decision to adjourn was made by the chairperson who was prompted to act by the lateness of the hour.

   _____

   _____

4. First the screws are screwed on at point B; next, the table is placed on its legs; and last, the screws at point C are tightened.

   _____

   _____

5. Advance cost recovery was abolished by Bill #B164. As a result, the consumers are assured that they are not required to pay for increases in cost of fuel until a public hearing has been held on the matter.

   _____

   _____

   _____

EXERCISE 10   Writing in the Active Voice

Choose one of the theses below and restate it in the active voice. Next, expand it into a paragraph written in the active voice, using your own experiences and observations.

My money has been spent wisely (unwisely).
My value system has been established by my parents (friends, church).
Some people may be trapped by their feelings (environment, societal demands).
My health has been affected by my life style (my life style has been affected by my health).

Name _____ *Date* _____

EXERCISE 11   Revising Faulty Predication I

Sentences 1–5 have faulty predicates consisting of a linking verb and an adverbial clause. Underline the linking verb once, and the adverbial clause twice. Sentences 6–10 have faulty predicates consisting of a transitive verb and an adverbial clause. Underline the transitive verb once, and the adverbial clause twice. Revise the sentences for clarity, and write the revised sentences on the lines below.

EXAMPLE

A winner is when the fastest horse passes the finish line.

A winner is the fastest horse across the finish line.

1. A novel is when there are characters who develop through the story.

   _____

   _____

2. The reason for her success is because she is bright.

   _____

   _____

3. A crime is when you commit a felony.

   _____

   _____

4. The good grades are when he studies hard.

   _____

   _____

5. The purpose of his visit is because he wants to cheer you up.

   _____

   _____

6. I read where the bridge has dropped three inches on one side.

   _____

   _____

7. We heard where the third baseman left and was picked up by the Lions.

   _____

   _____

8. George saw when the Wings won their first game.

_____

_____

9. The general manager told where the goalie was suffering a broken toe.

_____

_____

10. Joe never believes when the Wings win.

_____

_____

EXERCISE 12   Revising Faulty Predication II

In the following sentences, the subject and predicate do not relate logically to each other. Underline the predicate. Revise the sentence for clarity. Write the revised sentence on the lines below.

EXAMPLE
Prue's batting average is <u>better than Susan.</u>

Prue's batting average is better than
Susan's.

1. Nursing dislikes a sloppy student.

_____

_____

2. The buildings in New York are higher than Paris.

_____

_____

3. The starting place of a paper is organization.

_____

_____

4. Narrowing my topic became a total blank.

_____

_____

5. College is a matter of getting your financial statistics in order.

_____

_____

Name _____ *Date* _____

EXERCISE 13   Revising for Parallelism

In the following sentences or sentence groups, underline the nonparallel unit that needs revision. Revise the sentence so as to achieve parallelism. Write the sentence on the lines below.

EXAMPLE

An example of an inappropriate effect would be that the person would laugh while stating how upset he is at someone's death. An example of an appropriate effect would be matching emotion and expression.

An example of an inappropriate effect would be a person's laughing while stating how upset he is at someone's death. An example of an appropriate effect would be a person's crying while stating how upset he is.

1. The court trial and plea bargaining are the two best ways of serving justice. In the court trial the lawyers present evidence that will prove to a jury that one side is correct. The accused will plead guilty to a charge other than the original one in plea bargaining as a result of an agreement of the lawyers.

   _____
   _____
   _____
   _____

2. The four major characteristics of schizophrenia are: 1) to live in a fantasy world, 2) two opposing emotions are felt at the same time, 3) schizophrenics have disturbances in thought association, and 4) to exhibit a blunt or flat effect.

   _____
   _____
   _____
   _____

3. Avoid fad diets. Eat well-balanced meals. Exercise should be taken everyday for you to be healthy.

_____

_____

_____

4. Going to the amusement park is fun. We can ride the ferris wheel. We can scream on the roller coaster and the big slide. The dodge-em cars are also fun and likewise the hot air balloons.

_____

_____

_____

5. Nervously looking about, she told me to go to the bank to take out my savings, and she was biting her fingernails.

_____

_____

Name _____ *Date* _____

EXERCISE 14   Recognizing and Revising Non-Coordinate Structures

In the following sentences, underline the non-parallel phrase or clause needing revision. Revise the sentence to achieve clarity. Write the revised sentence on the lines below.

EXAMPLE

Lay midwives are virtually illegal in some states and <u>not enough programs</u> <u>to train them.</u>

There are not enough programs to train lay midwives; and they are virtually illegal in some states.

1. All reporters have their favorite stories, but don't necessarily reflect reality.

_____

_____

2. I don't like to mow the lawn, wash the car, or the leaves dropping in the fall.

_____

_____

3. In some cases it is noted that the child reaches out to bring the mother back and strong objections and emotional reactions such as crying.

_____

_____

_____

4. It is important that the nurse gives psychological counseling and to help the woman to cope with her psychological needs.

_____

_____

5. Peter, Buffie and with Aunt Lydia went down to the dock.

_____

_____

EXERCISE 15   Revising Sentences in Your Own Writing

Write a short paper on the following subject. Use your newly found skill in revising sentences to craft the sentences in your essay.

Imagine that the following is the astrological advice given for your birthday; moreover, imagine that you believe in astrological predictions. In your paper discuss how you would change or direct your actions now and for the coming year as a result of this advice.

Today's Birthday Advice: Don't be a stick-in-the-mud. Keep your suitcase packed for most of the year. Rearrange your living quarters, doing something to brighten them up. A few new friends will help, too. Really break out of the rut in September. Travel in June and have a ball.

11

CHOOSING EFFECTIVE WORDS

Choosing the right word to convey your meaning will be easier after you discover what makes words effective and under what conditions words become confusing.

Choosing Words for Clarity (20a)

Generalized words and phrases, groups of nouns that modify nouns, and words imprecisely or unidiomatically used make prose difficult to read.

Specific and Concrete Words

Generalized words, phrases, and statements are necessary in order to introduce, summarize, or conclude, but writing which contains only generalizations produces a vague message. Details, illustrations, and data support generalizations, develop ideas, and engage the reader's feelings. An overly general paragraph can be strengthened by using concrete or specific words or phrases with or in place of a general word or phrase:

> As I read through the articles, I noticed that my speed in reading each article varied. In the first, I was slowed by the large amount of statistical information; in the second, by technical terms. I brought a better background to the first than to the second.

revised to include detail:

> As I read through *"Casualties"* and *"Halley's Comet,"* I noticed that my speed in reading each article differed, *the first, taking five minutes and the second, fifteen.* In *"Casualties"* I was slowed by the large amount of statistical information, *which included figures on the relationship of poverty, unemployment, and childhood pregnancy to infant mortality.* In *"Halley's Comet"* the obstacles to rapid reading were the *large numbers of technical terms such as "perihelion," "elongated elliptical orbit," and "less predictable non-gravitational forces."* I brought a background *from my sociology classes to "Casualties" which made the article easier to read,* whereas *my weak* background *in astronomy* made *"Halley's Comet" difficult to understand.*

Nouns as Modifiers

Nouns that modify other nouns (nominal attributes) can confuse or slow down readers if they exist in a string of more than two nouns. Sentences that have series of nominal attributes can be revised by changing one of the nouns to a verbal, by dropping an unnecessary noun, or by rewording the sentence:

> The *computer research expansion block* voted against the bill.
>   can be revised to:
> The block favoring the expanding of computer research voted against the bill. (or) The block favoring the expansion of computer research voted against the bill.

Using the Exact Word

Words that sound similar or have the same root sometimes are confused:

> One *respect* of the report shows students improving.
>   should be:
> One *aspect* of the report shows students improving.

Idiomatic English

An idiom is a way of saying something that is characteristic of a language. Readers in a general audience can be slowed down or confused if the idiom the writer chooses is uncharacteristic of general usage in the language:

> I am *going by* my mother's house tonight. (regional usage)
> I am *going to* my mother's house tonight. (general usage)

Choosing Words for Emphasis   (20b)

Writing can be made emphatic and pointed by: 1) using verbals and verbs in place of nouns; 2) using active verbs in place of the verbs of being; 3) using fewer and shorter words. In addition, emphasis can be maintained by eliminating slang, dialect, euphemisms, clichés and other trite expressions, and shifts in the level of formality which might confuse or distract the reader.

Using Verbals and Verbs Instead of Nouns

Changing nouns to verbs or verbals can often make writing more emphatic:

> Her employer sees the necessity of an evaluation of her.
>   could be revised to:
> Her employer *must evaluate* her.

Using Emphatic Verbs

Writers composing or revising sentences should prefer verbs of action to verbs of being:

The inflation rate *is* higher this week.
   could be revised to:
The inflation rate *rose* this week. (or) The inflation rate *climbed* this week.

Using Fewer and Shorter Words

Writers who are composing or revising should prefer one word to several and short words to long ones. Long words or a group of words where one would have been sufficient will distract or bore the reader:

      REDUNDANT   UNNECESSARY
[*The truth is that*] [*I believe that*] the profession of physical therapist

      UNNECESSARY   LONG   UNNECESSARY
        GROUPS   WORD   WORD
[*tends to attract*] [*certain types of*] [*individuals*] [*characterized*]

                            UNNECESSARY
UNNECESSARY GROUP OF SHORT WORDS   LONG WORD
[*by a specific set of qualities that add up to*] [*an orientation*] *to* sensitivity and discipline.

   can be revised to:

The profession of physical therapy attracts sensitive and disciplined people.

Slang, Dialect, and Euphemism

Slang or *dialect* words mark the writer as part of a particular group or as from a particular region. The use of slang and dialect is appropriate when the audience is intimate and familiar with the terms. A general audience, however, finds dialect and slang distracting and sometimes confusing. An added problem is that slang, dialect, and euphemisms are often *clichés* (see below for a discussion of clichés):

Dear Sir,
   I am pleased to recommend John Jensen as a candidate for the American Scholarship Program. He gives evidence of considerable academic promise, and is *a great guy*.

                                         Yours truly,

Euphemisms are the polite kinds of words that writers use to refer to matters that are socially taboo. The subjects of sex, bodily elimination, death, and significant social and physical differences support clusters of euphemisms. Although occasionally appropriate, euphemisms are more often wordy and indirect.

   Your assessment of your audience, purpose, and medium will indicate whether you write:

Parnella is poor.   (or)   Parnella comes from a low socioeconomic group.

But the following sentence is wordy and indirect:

The economically deprived senior citizens living in the low-income areas of the city live in the midst of crime and are frequently victims of it.

can be revised to:

Older people living downtown are often attacked and robbed.

Unnecessary Variety

Although some variety in word choice is desirable, unnecessary variety distracts and sometimes confuses the reader. In an attempt to find variety, writers sometimes choose words that do not fit the level of formality, that draw attention to themselves because they are unusual, or that carry a different meaning from that intended:

The *parents'* anonymous group enables *parents* to discuss their *children* without the *children* present.

was unsuccessfully revised to:

The parents' anonymous group enables *progenitors* to discuss their children without the *juveniles* present.

Progenitors is an unusual word that usually means *predecessors*, rarely *parents; juveniles* normally has the meaning of *young person* or *youth* and does not connote relationship within a family.

A better revision retains one repeated word and substitutes a pronoun for the other:

The *parents'* anonymous group enables *parents* to discuss their children without them present.

Figurative Language

Figurative language, such as *metaphors, similes, personification, hyperbole,* and *puns,* adds variety to writing; however, its main use is to add meaning to ideas or to call attention to them.

• *Simile.* A simile makes an explicit comparison between two things, using the words *like* and *as* to signal that the comparison will follow:

The fullback extended his left hand *like a shy teenager curling his arm around his girl* and held the ball to his side.

• *Metaphor.* A metaphor makes an implicit comparison between two things:

The *nomadic* life of a news reporter suits Cheryl. When she was a child, she had loved to *roam* from city to city with her father. Now, she sets up her media *tent* wherever news is happening.

• *Personification.* A personification invests an inanimate object with living characteristics. The object, as a result, becomes like a plant, animal, or human:

The *city* is *proud* of its heritage and *smiles* benignly on its ethnic mix.

• *Hyperbole*. An hyperbole is a deliberate overstatement made in an attempt to dramatize an idea:

Give me the published novels of Agatha Christie, and *I will disappear into my easy chair for the rest of the year.*

• *Pun*. A pun is a play on words that sound similar. It has entertainment value and in certain instances gives a double meaning to an idea:

Foul, foul, he cried as he ran after the thieving goose.

Sometimes metaphors and similes become confused because their comparisons are not precisely made. Many of these mixed similes and metaphors emerge from clichéd metaphors and similes, comparisons that have been so overused that their essential point of similarity has been forgotten. Hyperboles, in addition, are often confused or overused metaphors or similes.

• *Confused simile:*

Her makeup was like *icing on a cake,* the rouge and eye color covering a myriad of wrinkles and sags. (cake and a myriad of wrinkles and sags are not comparable)

• *Confused hyperbole which is also a metaphor:*

The hurricane was the *last straw. (straw* in the proverb was the infinitesimal weight added to the camel's already heavy load, which made it unbearable and *broke the camel's back)*

Clichés and Trite Expressions

A *cliché* is an expression used so often that it has lost its freshness. Often clichés are metaphors that through overuse lose their meaning. *Trite expressions*, like clichés, have become so commonly used that they are boring and vague:

TRITE

I have a *meaningful relationship* with my job, and the money I am paid

CLICHÉ

for working is just *out of this world.*
could be revised to:
I enjoy working, and my wages are high.

Choosing Words That Do Not Discriminate   (20c)

Words that imply judgments about the gender, racial, physical, and social differences among people are often part of the writer's unconscious language habits. Since such judgments not only distract and anger readers but also perpetuate discrimination, writers should recognize and avoid them. Sometimes *discriminatory* words appear as unnecessary (gratuitous) modifiers pointing out differences between the person referred to and other members of a group:

> Ballard, *an Arab* real estate broker, has been indicted for taking bribes.
>   should be revised to:
> Ballard, a real estate broker, has been indicted for taking bribes.

Words also discriminate by referring to persons with terms either implicitly demeaning or considered so by them:

> The *girls* in our office work hard.
>   should be:
> The *women* in our office work hard.

Pronouns sometimes show discrimination by referring to a generic term such as *human being* or *doctor* as if it were exclusively male when it actually includes both genders:

> A *doctor* must study all of his life.

Changing the generic term to plural, rewording the sentence, or using *his* or *her* or *he* or *she* will eliminate the gender discrimination:

> *Doctors* must study all *their* lives. (or) A *doctor* spends a lifetime studying.

Exercise Objectives

Recognizing and using concrete modifiers, verbs of action, and figurative language; eliminating long strings of words, confused words, euphemisms, slang, dialect, clichés, trite expressions, and ineffective repetition.

11 CHOOSING EFFECTIVE WORDS _____

Name _____ *Date* _____

EXERCISE 1 Adding Concrete Modifiers

The underlined words and phrases will be less confusing or vague after the addition of concrete modifiers. Substitute or add clauses, phrases, or words that make the sentence clearer. Write the revised sentence on the lines below.

EXAMPLE
My instructor boasts considerable <u>knowledge.</u>

My instructor boasts considerable knowledge
about snakes, insects, and Shakespeare.

1. Even though most boys like camping, my brother doesn't like the <u>inconvenience.</u>

   _____

   _____

   _____

2. <u>This book</u> is filled with <u>information.</u>

   _____

   _____

   _____

3. <u>Maturation</u> occurs <u>early.</u>

   _____

   _____

   _____

4. Your <u>speech on revenge</u> spurred me to do <u>some writing.</u>

   _____

   _____

   _____

5. <u>Education</u> must demand <u>more</u> of its <u>students.</u>

   _____

   _____

   _____

EXERCISE 2   Revising Long Series of Noun Modifiers

The following sentences contain strings of nouns modifying nouns (nominal attributes). Underline the nominal attributes and the noun they modify. Revise the sentences to eliminate the wordiness, and write the revision on the lines below.

EXAMPLE
Donald and Kathy had a <u>flirtation type encounter</u>.

Donald and Kathy had a flirtation.

1. You can put together the option equipment package you want.

_____

_____

_____

2. The economy has an inflation orientation outlook.

_____

_____

_____

3. The voice audition process finally ended.

_____

_____

_____

4. Minority venture capital will be provided by the new fund.

_____

_____

_____

5. My research task was to examine Christian belief ritual formats in the state of Kentucky.

_____

_____

Name ————————————————— *Date* ————————

EXERCISE 3   Recognizing Confused Words

The following sentences contain words that have been confused with a similar word. Look up the underlined word in the dictionary to establish its meaning. Write a sentence on the line below in which it is used appropriately.

EXAMPLE
The <u>disparate</u> thieves escaped in my car.

Their disparate value systems ultimately led to a conflict.

1. The vacation had an invigorating <u>affect</u> on her.

  —————————————————————————

2. My girlfriend is <u>disinterested</u> in my broken ankle.

  —————————————————————————

3. The wind <u>disbursed</u> the seeds.

  —————————————————————————

4. There were three <u>incidence</u> of violence at the game.

  —————————————————————————

5. He gave an account of his <u>factitious</u> journey.

  —————————————————————————

6. That is the most <u>practicable</u> jacket I have yet seen! I hope there is one left in the store for me.

  —————————————————————————

  —————————————————————————

7. I am <u>adverse</u> to going with you.

  —————————————————————————

8. On a separate sheet of paper, create sentences in which you use the following words appropriately: *complement, biennial, capitol, elicit, funereal, respectably, urbane, parameter.*

EXERCISE 4   Identifying Idioms

In the following sentences, a preposition is needed to complete the idiomatic expression. Look up the underlined word in the dictionary for the preposition generally used with it.

EXAMPLE

Henry was <u>oblivious</u> ___*of*___ me and the passage of time.

1. Louisa was <u>capable</u> _____ handling the bulldozer.

2. Barrett had a great <u>distaste</u> _____ squid.

3. Martha had a strong <u>dislike</u> _____ liver.

4. Don't <u>compare</u> Martha's taste _____ Barrett's.

5. You don't have to <u>comply</u> _____ the schedule.

EXERCISE 5   Using Verbs or Verbals Instead of Nouns

In the sentences below when appropriate replace a noun with a verb or verbal.

EXAMPLE

Sheila is beginning the establishment of an *ad hoc* committee.

Sheila is establishing an ad hoc committee.

1. The deans decided on the continuation of the program.

_____

_____

2. The project improved in manageability under Joanne's guidance.

_____

_____

3. The professor agrees to the acceptability of the importance of ritual.

_____

_____

4. The paper has a need of revision.

_____

_____

5. The seminar on portfolio management has the goal of informing people how to invest.

_____

_____

Name _____ *Date* _____

EXERCISE 6 Using Verbs of Action

The following sentences contain verbs of being. Underline the verbs of being, and then change them to verbs of action. Write the revised sentence on the line below.

EXAMPLE

I <u>am</u> in the men's chorus.

I sing in the men's chorus.

1. The autumn colors this year are brilliant orange, yellow, and red, colors dazzling to the eye.

_____

_____

2. Though he was always a great humorist in his writings, Thurber was irascible when he was older.

_____

_____

_____

3. Before the week was over, he was dead.

_____

4. Black cherry ice cream is a good-tasting ice cream.

_____

5. She was a candidate for governor.

_____

EXERCISE 7 Revising with Fewer and Shorter Words

The sentences below contain many unnecessary words and some long words that can be replaced by short words. Revise each group. Write the revisions on the lines below.

EXAMPLE

We are all of a like mind with our employer at this point in time.

Now we agree with our employer.

_____

1. It is probably safe to assume that nearly everyone has an aspect of his personality which departs severely from everyone else's and is also antithetical in regard to tastes and viewpoints to other aspects of his or her personality.

_____

_____

_____

2. Secondly, given the nature of this essay, specifically, and the limited time and space constraints in which I necessarily work, generally, my vagueness about specifics is inevitable. I trust, however, that this will not prove troublesome to read.

_____

_____

_____

3. The fact is that I am not a typical listener of classical music because there is indeed another musical genre on my list, heavy rock, sometimes known as "heavy-metal." Of course, coexistence between the two styles may seem impossible, but the opposite is true. The resulting effect of their assault on my senses invigorates me so that I maintain the energy level necessary in order to perform my daily tasks.

_____

_____

_____

4. Because of the fact that the statement in respect to the educational institution is negative, I will retire from the room.

_____

_____

5. In the case of a breakdown of a public vehicle, all passengers will be compensated for their bus fare. Children, however, will be transported to school free of charge in a board of education motorized attendance module.

_____

_____

_____

Name _____ *Date* _____

EXERCISE 8   Revising to Eliminate Slang, Dialect, and Euphemisms

Revise the following sentences so as to eliminate slang, dialect, or euphemisms that might distract the reader. Write the revised sentence on the line below.

EXAMPLE
With the subtleties of genetic engineering, changes in processing, and new food sources including the gunk that is added, the term "natural" is meaningless.

With the subtleties of genetic engineering, changes in processing, and new food sources including all the additives, the term "natural" is meaningless.

1. Companies are very specific about the management experience they want. Gals are being scrutinized for the same exacting qualifications as guys.

_____

_____

_____

2. A realist is a person who lives comfortably off the interest accumulating from the capital, capital which is actually the result of energy and vision invested by some sucker living in a previous generation.

_____

_____

_____

3. Students living on campus have advantages over students living at home. They don't get stuck at home with their parents but can study with their friends in the dormitory.

_____

_____

_____

4. Alex Haley is a member of a racial minority.

_____

_____

5. Everybody in this room should get off their butts and go to work.

_____

_____

6. My problem is stalling out, probably the fault of a rotten gasket, and my second problem is a new wrinkle of the first.

_____

_____

7. There must be a little girl's room in the restaurant.

_____

_____

8. Ida rests in peace; she now lives only in our memories.

_____

_____

9. The democratization of the country came from the elimination of the rival elements through the intervention of a friendly military task force.

_____

_____

_____

10. The entire expedition tossed its cookies on the flight over the Rocky Mountains.

_____

_____

11 CHOOSING EFFECTIVE WORDS

Name _____ *Date* _____

EXERCISE 9   Eliminating Clichés and Trite Expressions

Underline clichés and trite expressions. Revise the sentence by removing the cliché and providing concrete, new words or phrases. Write the revised sentence on the line below.

EXAMPLE

I have <u>been bitten by a bug</u> known as <u>the root of all evil.</u>

I am greedy for money.

1. The Soviet government was asked to apologize but flunked the test.

   _____

   _____

2. Education is the life blood of civilization.

   _____

   _____

3. There are many pleasures in life just too good for words.

   _____

   _____

4. She has her foot in the door for a good grade because the teacher is her cousin.

   _____

   _____

5. Last semester, when I didn't have my nose to the grindstone, I was burning the midnight oil.

   _____

   _____

EXERCISE 10 Eliminating Ineffective Repetition of Words

In the following sentence groups, underline the words repeated. Revise ineffective repetition by finding a synonym that does not distract or confuse the reader, by eliminating words, or by sentence combining. Write the revised sentences on the line below. (See chapter 9, exercises 14 and 15 for effective repetition of words and patterns.)

EXAMPLE

Many parents have never <u>communicated</u> with their children about sex. As a result, no <u>communication</u> has occurred about contraception. It isn't until the fact is <u>communicated</u> to the parents and the girl that a baby is on the way that either of them talks about sex.

Many parents don't communicate with their children about sex, and, as a result, their children don't know about contraceptives. In fact, it isn't until the parents and their daughter find that she is pregnant that they talk about sex at all.

1. We are developing groups to plan future development of the Proctor Project.

_____

2. The orchestration of setting, singing, and orchestra was masterful.

_____

3. Health food addicts think that only certain foods are healthful. For a healthy body, they recommend a diet of fruits, nuts, and juices.

_____

4. Rich and Richfield and Company, a company that has only rich clients, has relocated in Suite D.

_____

5. She says that if she pursues a career in nursing, then it will be as a geriatric nurse which is a nurse who works with the elderly.

_____

_____

Name ─────────────────────────── Date ───────────

EXERCISE 11   Recognizing Figurative Language

Each of the sentences below contains figurative language. Underline the figure and identify it in the space above.

EXAMPLE

personification

A U.S. tank <u>sprang to life</u>, firing into the hill.

1. Helicopters whirl like spiders over the water.

2. He measures out his love to his family as if he were serving boiled potatoes.

3. The tiny two-cylinder motors whined across the water like mosquitoes.

4. Tell me you love me and I will write your name in the sky!

5. When she is offered a cigarette, a red light flashes on for her and she stops.

6. Since the President began wearing a hearing device, the Hearing Industries Association has been up to its ears in orders.

7–10 Write on the lines below sentences containing figurative language which is clear and not clichéd. Look for examples in your own and your classmates' writing. Identify the kind of figure directly above it.

7. _____

_____

8. _____

_____

9. _____

_____

10. _____

_____

EXERCISE 12   Finding Effective Figures of Speech

The sentences below contain confused or clichéd metaphors, similes, and hyperboles. Underline the ineffective figure of speech and either devise a fresh and more accurate one to replace it or revise the sentence to clarify the meaning.

EXAMPLE

She looked <u>fresh as a daisy</u>; she smelled <u>sweet as a rose</u>.

She looked as fresh as the new leaflets of mint in grandmother's herb garden, and she smelled as good.

1. The hotbed of rumor came right out of the horse's mouth.

_____

_____

2. Jessica was cool as a cucumber as she turned on her heel away from the crowd.

_____

_____

3. What if you were in the shoes of that unfortunate deer?

_____

_____

4. If he votes against Proposal B, Vernon is not worth his salt.

_____

_____

5. Unemployment threw us a curve ball and took our marriage for a ride.

_____

_____

11   CHOOSING EFFECTIVE WORDS _____

Name _____ *Date* _____

EXERCISE 13   Eliminating Discriminatory Language I

Underline discriminatory words or phrases in the following sentences. Write a revised sentence on the line below.

EXAMPLE

Only <u>the wives of lawyers</u> know about their secret fears.

Only the spouses of lawyers know about their secret fears.

1. Cranston is an efficient, black lady dean.

   _____

   _____

2. The working wife and her husband had left the child alone.

   _____

   _____

3. How many man-hours of work did the lady plumber complete?

   _____

   _____

4. Among all the working men interviewed, a divorcee had the most to say about working conditions.

   _____

   _____

5. Jim, a victim of cerebral palsy, swims with me.

   _____

   _____

EXERCISE 14 Eliminating Discriminatory Language II

The following sentences imply a gender discrimination through the personal pronoun. Revise the sentences by using *he or she,* rewording them, or changing the pronoun and its antecedent to plural.

EXAMPLE

A good cook always enjoys preparing her family's Thanksgiving dinner.

Good cooks always enjoy preparing their family's Thanksgiving dinner.

1. I kicked all of her tires to test her state of disrepair.

2. The average pioneer left his homeland, never to see it again.

3. Why can't man keep the peace, when he can create so many technical marvels?

4. A nurse must be sensitive to changes in her patients.

5. Early man had several tools that he used for hunting, fishing, and grinding corn.

EXERCISE 15 Eliminating Discriminatory Language from Your Own Writing

Write a short paper or a long paragraph on a separate sheet of paper on one of the following topics. As you write, consciously avoid using discriminatory terms. Your audience should be a sympathetic adult, and your purpose is to expose unfair treatment.

The average student's response to exam week
How teachers influence students
How I feel about doctors (nurses, bill collectors, etc.)

11 CHOOSING EFFECTIVE WORDS _____

Name _____ *Date* _____

EXERCISE 16   Revising for Effective Word Use: Review

Underline words and phrases in the following sentences and sentence groups that are 1) confusing, vague, or difficult to read; 2) inappropriate or boring; 3) complicated; or 4) discriminatory. Revise to eliminate those words and phrases. Write the revised sentences on the lines below.

1. Volunteers manned the registration booth.

_____

_____

2. Anybody knows how much trouble he has cashing a personal check in a strange city.

_____

_____

3. We are very fond of our black neighbors.

_____

_____

4. The housewives should stand in this line; the working girls, in that one.

_____

_____

5. No one will hand you anything on a silver platter.

_____

_____

6. The adolescent misconception stereotypes were under discussion.

_____

_____

7. Shelley chimed in with a voice like a foghorn.

_____

_____

8. The reporters were ordered to structure the dissemination of information in accordance with prioritized communications objectives.

_____

_____

9. The committee gave the tasks of development to Joseph, who wasn't up to it.

_____

_____

10. Crews of workers depopulated chicken coops filled with infected chickens.

_____

_____

12

SPELLING

Your audience follows your writing more easily when it has no misspelled words. When spelling errors do occur, readers pause at the misspelled word before moving on. Although they probably figure out what word you meant to write, the error slows them down, and your writing is thus less efficient. The following guidelines will help you become a better speller, but the dictionary is the place to find confirmation of a correct spelling.

Common Spelling Patterns   (22b)

The following patterns will help you when you are undecided about spelling certain words. Although these patterns do have exceptions, they work often enough to make it worth your while to memorize them.

Words Containing *ie* or *ei*

If the vowel rhymes with *see*, write *i* before *e* except after *c*:

niece	field	relief
receive	ceiling	conceit

If the vowel rhymes with *pay*, write *e* before *i*:

neighbor	reign	beige

When the sound is neither *ee* nor *ay*, the vowel will usually be written with *e* before *i*:

foreign	Fahrenheit	heifer

Final *e* Before a Suffix

Drop the final silent *e* before adding a suffix that begins with a vowel but not before one that begins with a consonant:

love	lov*able*	lov*ing*	love*ly*
use	us*able*	us*ing*	use*less*
care	care*ful*	car*ing*	care*less*

237

The *e* is usually retained before suffixes beginning with *a* and *o* if the preceding consonant is a soft *c* or *g*; but the *e* is dropped, following the usual pattern, before *i*:

chan[ge]able   chan[g]ing
servi[ce]able   servi[c]ing

Changing *y* to *i*

If a word ends in a consonant followed by *y*, change the *y* to *i* before adding a suffix beginning with any letter except *i*. If a vowel precedes the *y* keep it:

stu[dy]   stu[di]*ed*   stu[di]*ous*   stu[dy]*ing*
love[ly]   love[li]*er*   love[li]*est*
st[ay]   st[ay]*ing*   st[ay]*ed*
dism[ay]   dism[ay]*ing*   dism[ay]*ed*

Doubling of Final Consonants

Double the final consonant before adding a suffix if the final consonant follows a single vowel and if it ends on an accented syllable:

forg[et]   forge*tt*ing   unforge*tt*able
pl[an]   pla*nn*ing   pla*nn*ed

The last consonant in *appear* is preceded by two vowels:

app[ear]   app*eared*   app*earance*

The last consonant in *turn* is preceded by a consonant:

tu[rn]   *turned*   *turning*

The accent in con*sid*er is not on the last syllable:

con[sid]er   consid*er*ed   consid*er*ing.

Doubled Letters with Prefixes and Suffixes

When the prefix of a word ends with the same letter that the main part of the word starts with or a suffix begins with the same letter the word ends with, remember to include both letters:

dis + similar   green + *ness*

-able and -ible

If the root of a word is itself an independent word, the suffix will usually be -able:

avail + *able*	laugh + *able*
avoid + *able*	profit + *able*

If the root of a word does not exist as an independent word, the ending is usually -ible:

infall + *ible*	terr + *ible*
cred + *ible*	divis + *ible*

The ending will usually be spelled -ible if the word ends in a double consonant that includes at least one *s*:

defens + *ible*	irrespons + *ible*
admiss + *ible*	permiss + *ible*

Distinguishing -ally and -ly

The suffix -ly is added to adjectives to form adverbs:

quick + *ly*	bright + *ly*	friend + *ly*

The suffix -ally is added to adjectives ending in -ic to form adverbs:

academic + *ally*	artistic + *ally*	basic + *ally*

Problems with Pronunciation   (22c)

Some words are misspelled because writers do not hear or pronounce some of the letters, and as a result, they do not include them in the spelling of the words.

Some letters are dropped from the ends of words, making the words resemble a correctly spelled word with a different meaning:

fin*d*	fine	six*th*	six	los*t*	loss	
alon*g*	alone	crow*d*	crow	bein*g*	been	
min*d*	mine	wen*t*	when	an*d*	an	am

Frequently Confused Words (22d)

Certain words sound the same or are similar but have different meanings and are spelled differently:

their	there	they're	its	it's
whose	who's		accept	except
affect	effect		all ready	already

Some words are exceptions to the spelling patterns and others are hard to revisualize correctly. The spelling of these words must be memorized or checked in the dictionary. A few of these words are:

occasion   necessary   graduate   adolescent   competent

Exercise Objectives

Understanding spelling patterns and reasons for incorrect spelling; recognizing the importance of the dictionary in spelling correctly; analyzing your own spelling errors.

Name _____ *Date* _____

EXERCISE 1   Spelling Words with *ie* or *ei*

On the following lines, write a sentence using the word to the left. Be certain you have spelled the word correctly, according to the first pattern on p. 237.

EXAMPLE

weight   *The weight of the Trucks damages the highway.*

believe	1. _____
friend	2. _____
ceiling	3. _____
achieve	4. _____
diesel	5. _____
grief	6. _____
freight	7. _____
either	8. _____
conceive	9. _____
neighbor	10. _____
neither	11. _____
Fahrenheit	12. _____
sleight-of-hand	13. _____
belief	14. _____
weight	15. _____

EXERCISE 2   Spelling Words with Final *e* Before a Suffix I

In the following blanks, write the word given in the margin adding the indicated suffix. Make certain that you have spelled the new form of the word correctly according to the second pattern on p. 237.

EXAMPLE

advise   -ed: *advised*

-ing: *advising*

-able: *advisable*

amuse   **1.** -ing: _____

-ment: _____

argue   **2.** -ing: _____

-ment: _____

believe   **3.** -ing: _____

-able: _____

come   **4.** -ing: _____

change   **5.** -ing: _____

-ed: _____

-able: _____

hope   **6.** -ing: _____

-less: _____

arrive   **7.** -ing: _____

-al: _____

notice   **8.** -ing: _____

-able: _____

desire   **9.** -ing: _____

-able: _____

-ous: _____

love   **10.** -ing: _____

-ed: _____

-able: _____

EXERCISE 3   Spelling Words with Final *e* Before a Suffix II

In the blanks below, write the word listed at the left with the indicated suffix added. Make certain that you spell the new form correctly according to the second pattern on p. 237.

EXAMPLE

care   -ful: *careful*

      -less: *careless*

excite   **1.** -ment: _____

safe   **2.** -ly: _____

      -ty: _____

sure   **3.** -ly: _____

      -ty: _____

bare   **4.** -ly: _____

      -ness: _____

amuse   **5.** -ment: _____

hope   **6.** -less: _____

      -ful: _____

sincere   **7.** -ly: _____

extreme   **8.** -ly: _____

awe   **9.** -some: _____

arrange   **10.** -ment: _____

EXERCISE 4   Changing *y* to *i*

In the blanks below, write the words listed on the left with the indicated syllable added. Make certain that you have spelled the word correctly according to the first pattern on p. 238.

EXAMPLE

beauty -ful: *beautiful*   easy   -er: *easier*

-ly: *easily*

-est: *easiest*

monkey **1.** -ed with _____   angry **6.** -ly: _____

-ing around _____   -est: _____

delay **2.** -ed: _____   funny **7.** -er: _____

-ing: _____   -est: _____

busy **3.** -er: _____   lady **8.** -like: _____

-est: _____   -ship: _____

ugly **4.** -ly: _____   happy **9.** -er: _____

-ness: _____   -est: _____

-er: _____   -ly: _____

marry **5.** -ed: _____   merry **10.** -er: _____

-ing: _____   -est: _____

Name _____ *Date* _____

EXERCISE 5   Doubling Final Consonants

In the blanks below, write the word listed to the left with the indicated suffix added. Make certain that the new form is spelled correctly according to the second pattern on p. 238.

EXAMPLE

plan   -ing: *planning*
        -ed: *planned*

confer   **1.** -ing: _____   prefer   **5.** -ing: _____
         -ed: _____   -ed: _____

admit   **2.** -ed: _____   occur   **6.** -ed: _____
         -ing: _____   -ing: _____
         -ance: _____   -ence: _____

man   **3.** -ed: _____   equip   **7.** -ed: _____
         -ish: _____   -ing: _____

drop   **4.** -ed: _____   red   **8.** -er: _____
         -ing: _____   -est: _____
                                                      -en: _____

EXERCISE 6 Leaving Final Consonants Undoubled

On the blanks below, write the words listed to the left with the indicated suffix added. Make certain that the new form is spelled correctly according to the second pattern on p. 238.

EXAMPLE

train   -ed: _*trained*_

         -ing: _*training*_

         -er: _*trainer*_

         -ee: _*trainee*_

bend   1. -ed: _____   need   4. -y: _____

           -ing: _____   -ed: _____

                                          -ing: _____

insist   2. -ed: _____   wonder   5. -ed: _____

           -ing: _____   -ing: _____

remain   3. -ed: _____

           -ing: _____

EXERCISE 7 Spelling Words with Doubled Letters

On the blanks below, write the words to the left with the indicated prefix or suffix added. Make certain you have spelled the word correctly according to the third pattern on p. 238.

EXAMPLE

book   -keeping: _*bookkeeping*_

green	1. -ness: _____		brown	11. -ness: _____
clean	2. -ness: _____		satisfied	12. dis-: _____
named	3. un-: _____		numbered	13. un-: _____
shapen	4. mis-: _____		wool	14. -ly: _____
necessary	5. un-: _____		cool	15. -ly: _____
cruel	6. -ly: _____		hold	16. with-: _____
drunken	7. -ness: _____		sudden	17. -ness: _____
spell	8. mis-: _____		news	18. -stand: _____
moral	9. -ly: _____		over	19. -ride: _____
over	10. -run: _____		relation	20. inter-: _____

Name _____ *Date* _____

EXERCISE 8   Spelling Words with *-able*

Check the words in the margin to see whether the base word is a full word or would be a full word except for a final *e*. Then, spell the word with the *-able* added. Finally, think of two additional words that end with *-able* and write them on the lines below.

EXAMPLE

believ(e)   *believable*

accept	1. _____	comfort	7. _____
pass	2. _____	perish	8. _____
work	3. _____	laugh	9. _____
consider	4. _____	size	10. _____
excus(e)	5. _____		11. _____
fashion	6. _____		12. _____

EXERCISE 9   Spelling Words with *-ible*

Using the base given to the left, complete the word with *-ible*. Write the completed word on the line to the right.

EXAMPLE

divis   *divisible*

feas	1. _____
aud	2. _____
indel	3. _____
cred	4. _____
vis	5. _____
sens	6. _____
respons	7. _____
permiss	8. _____
incomprehens	9. _____
poss	10. _____

EXERCISE 10   Spelling Words with -*ally* and -*ly*

Change the words below by adding -*ly* to form an adverb or adding -*ally* to form an adverb from an adjective ending in *ic*.

EXAMPLE

basic   *basically*

usual   1. _____   dramatic   9. _____

joyful   2. _____   scientific   10. _____

sad   3. _____   foolish   11. _____

academic   4. _____   weird   12. _____

cold   5. _____   frantic   13. _____

warm   6. _____   scholastic   14. _____

direct   7. _____   slow   15. _____

aesthetic 8. _____

Name _____ Date _____

EXERCISE 11 Review Exercises I

Ask a classmate or your teacher to read each of the following words and the sentence in which it is used. On a separate sheet of paper write the sentence and underline the particular word reviewed. Make certain that *all* of the words in the sentence are spelled correctly.

1. receive . . . The congregation *receives* her blessing.
2. receipt . . . He gave me a *receipt* for the money.
3. heir . . . His son was the only *heir* to his fortune.
4. ceiling . . . The plaster on the *ceiling* is cracked.
5. deceived . . . The thief *deceived* the elderly man.
6. studious . . . The child seems *studious*.
7. humidifier . . . The *humidifier* malfunctioned.
8. dismayed . . . My mother was *dismayed* at the state of his room.
9. easiest . . . The *easiest* lesson is the last one.
10. angrily . . . The man seized the dog *angrily*.
11. lovable . . . The weird little man is *lovable*.
12. excitement . . . The long freight train caused much *excitement*.
13. biting . . . The mosquitoes are *biting* tonight.
14. desirable . . . The most *desirable* acreage is across the road.
15. careful . . . He should be *careful* when he is dyeing his hair.
16. extremely . . . Joseph is *extremely* secretive about his business.
17. usable . . . The *usable* parts of the motor should be saved.
18. useless . . . The *useless* parts can be thrown away.
19. arguing . . . The children have been *arguing* all day.
20. doubly . . . I felt *doubly* mortified by the second remark.

EXERCISE 12   Review Exercises II

Ask a classmate or your teacher to read each of the following words and the sentence in which it is used. On a separate sheet of paper write the sentence and underline the particular word reviewed. Make certain that all words in the sentence are spelled correctly.

1. unforgettable . . . The ninth inning was *unforgettable.*
2. planning . . . The teams are *planning* another series next year.
3. transferred . . . She has probably been *transferred* to another ward.
4. appeared . . . The doctor's judgment *appeared* to be sound.
5. persisted . . . The man *persisted* in turning the wrong way.
6. conferring . . . The umpire and the manager are *conferring.*
7. preferring . . . *Preferring* the loveliest garden, we came here.
8. occurred . . . The mistake *occurred* only once.
9. admittance . . . They couldn't gain *admittance* to the bar.
10. written . . . She had *written* her name for the first time.
11. bookkeeping . . . I dropped my *bookkeeping* class.
12. unnumbered . . . The pages in the manuscript were *unnumbered.*
13. illiterate . . . What percentage of applicants is *illiterate?*
14. unnecessary . . . The incident was *unnecessary.*
15. misunderstanding . . . It arose from a *misunderstanding.*
16. roommate . . . My *roommate* is in conference with his counselor.
17. withhold . . . The registration office can *withhold* my credit.
18. misbehave . . . Connie *misbehaves* in school.
19. dissatisfied . . . We are *dissatisfied* with the coach service.
20. unbelievable . . . They told me an *unbelievable* story.
21. sensible . . . She made a *sensible* judgment.
22. profitable . . . We thought the business would be *profitable.*
23. inseparable . . . Keith and Kenneth are *inseparable* companions.
24. incredible . . . The speed of the surgeons was *incredible.*
25. responsible . . . Who is *responsible* for this mistake?
26. absolutely . . . You are *absolutely* right!
27. pessimistically . . . My aunt views life *pessimistically.*
28. artistically . . . The beads were hung *artistically.*
29. occasionally . . . *Occasionally,* rifle shots could be heard.
30. usually . . . We don't *usually* answer the phone this late.

Name _____ Date _____

EXERCISE 13 Choosing the Right Spelling

In the following blanks, fill in the appropriate word of the two indicated above each section.

fine or find

EXAMPLE

Did you __*find*__ the telephone number?

1. She has a _____ sense of color.

2. Did you _____ your socks?

3. The brush has very _____ bristles.

4. I can't _____ the aspirin.

5. You look _____ today.

mine or mind

1. I don't _____ her calling me.

2. Those cookies are _____.

3. Why don't you make up your _____?

4. Do you _____ if I look at your book?

5. The sweater she wore Wednesday was _____.

alone or along

1. I went walking _____ the beach _____.

2. I would rather be left _____.

3. Daisies and wild roses grow _____ the highway.

4. I am _____ again!

5. The problems go _____ with the job.

crow or crowd

1. The _____ was very noisy.

2. The _____ is a large glossy black bird.

mole or mold

3. He had a _____ on his chin.

4. I wanted to _____ the clay with my own hands.

5. A _____ is a small mammal that lives underground.

loss or lost

1. The Pistons _____ the game.

2. The _____ moved them down to third place.

3. The players' _____ of prestige was worse than their _____ of salary.

4. The doll had been _____ in the park.

5. The _____ of her bike resulted in the _____ of her paper route.

an, am, or and

1. _____ apple _____ a piece of cheese made up my lunch.

2. I _____ still hungry.

3. You _____ I make a perfect couple.

4. _____ angry citizen _____ _____ irritable bus driver caused the problem.

5. Do you know who I _____?

the or then   then or them   when or went

1. She saw _____ crawling out of _____ space craft.

2. _____, who did commit the crime? Who robbed _____?

3. He _____ home _____ the party was over.

4. I _____ to class late.

5. _____ have you ever gone to class early?

been or being

1. The teacher is _____ very patient.

2. He has _____ patient for a long time.

3. _____ gentle with the kitten is difficult for a two-year-old.

4. You have _____ waiting for a long time.

5. Who has _____ eating my share of the cookies?

12 SPELLING ――――――――――――――――

EXERCISE 14   Choosing the Right Word I

In the following sentences, place the correct form of *their*, *there*, or *they're* in the blank. Before you start, read the definitions of these words below.

> *Their* indicates possession: They wore *their* coats.
> *There* indicates where something is: Their coats are *there*.
> *They're* is a contraction of they are: *They're* (they are) on their way.

EXAMPLE

They're good people.

1. My children always tell me where ――――――― going.

2. ――――――― are fifteen students in a class.

3. ――――――― weird.

4. I don't know whether ――――――― good or bad.

5. ――――――― they are!

6. The chalk is over ―――――――.

7. The squirrel is up ―――――――.

8. ――――――― is the Purdy Library, over ―――――――, across the Mall.

9. ――――――― driving ――――――― cars too fast.

10. Over ――――――― is the bus ――――――― taking to go back to ―――――
    hometown.

EXERCISE 15   Choosing the Right Word II

In the following sentences, place the correct form of *its* or *it's* in the blank. Before you start, read the definitions of these words below.

> *Its* indicates possession: The tree lost *its* leaves.
> *It's* is a contraction of it is: *It's* (it is) over there.

EXAMPLE

Its a big school.

1. Since the summer is over, ――――――― too late to buy a swim suit.

2. ――――――― too much to take.

3. ――――――― a bird; ――――――― a plane; no, ――――――― Superman.

4. I don't know where ――――――― going.

5. _____ feathers are wet.

6. Where is _____ nest?

7. Perhaps _____ mother has pushed it out of the nest.

8. The idea has lost _____ force.

9. _____ bark is worse than _____ bite.

10. _____ wagging _____ tail.

EXERCISE 16   Choosing the Right Word III

In the following sentences, place the correct form of *whose* or *who's* in the blank. Before you start, read the definitions of these words below.

Whose indicates possession: *Whose* books are those?
Who's is a contraction of who is: *Who's* the boy?

EXAMPLE

Who's there?

1. _____ your teacher this semester?

2. Gloria is the one _____ typing is the best.

3. Where is the girl _____ going with me?

4. I am the girl _____ going with you.

5. He is the man _____ car you pushed to the gas station.

Name _____ Date _____

EXERCISE 17   Spelling the Exceptions to the Patterns

Some words are difficult to spell because they are exceptions to the spelling patterns. The best way to remember the spellings is to memorize them. For each of the words below, write a short sentence in which you use the word spelled correctly.

EXAMPLE

acknowledgment   *I received an acknowledgment of the check.*

argument   1. _____

awful   2. _____

doubly   3. _____

incredibly   4. _____

judgment   5. _____

ninth   6. _____

possibly   7. _____

probably   8. _____

truly   9. _____

wisdom   10. _____

advantageous   11. _____

courageous

12. _____

_____

marriageable

13. _____

_____

noticeable

14. _____

_____

serviceable

15. _____

_____

dyeing

16. _____

_____

acreage

17. _____

_____

herein

18. _____

_____

lineage

19. _____

_____

financier

20. _____

_____

Name ─────────────────────────────── Date ──────────

EXERCISE 18   Analyzing Your Own Patterns of Misspellings

Below are places for you to list the words you have misspelled in your essays and other class work.

1. _____   18. _____
2. _____   19. _____
3. _____   20. _____
4. _____   21. _____
5. _____   22. _____
6. _____   23. _____
7. _____   24. _____
8. _____   25. _____
9. _____   26. _____
10. _____   27. _____
11. _____   28. _____
12. _____   29. _____
13. _____   30. _____
14. _____   31. _____
15. _____   32. _____
16. _____   33. _____
17. _____   34. _____

Examine the words you have listed to see whether your misspellings form a pattern. Are they the result of the nonapplication of a standard pattern, the adding or dropping of letters incorrectly, the confusing of words that sound or look similar, or a cause unique to your writing? Describe the results of your analysis in a well-developed paragraph. *Reminder:* when you discuss a letter or a word, you underline it.

13

PUNCTUATING SENTENCES

The signals of punctuation help map writing for a reader, indicating when a sentence begins (a capital letter), when it ends (period, question mark, exclamation point), and how the parts of the sentence and the words in it are related to each other (commas, semicolons, quotation marks, underlinings, hyphens, capitals, and apostrophes). Since you will want to provide clear directions for your reader, make certain that you know the conventional marks of punctuation.

End Punctuation (23a)

Use end punctuation to signal the end of a sentence. The three end marks are a *period,* a *question mark,* and an *exclamation point:*

> The engine sounds noisy.
> Does the engine sound strange to you?
> That sounds like a broken fan belt!

Periods are the most commonly used end punctuation; occasionally, they can mark off a sentence fragment when you want to achieve a particular rhetorical effect:

> SENTENCE: There is only one man who had the motive, the opportunity, the technical knowledge, and the utter lack of humanity to kill poor Mrs. Sappington.
> FRAGMENTS: Only one man. Otis Armstrong.

Question Marks are used at the ends of sentences that are *direct* questions. (Indirect questions are embedded in *whether* or *if* clauses and are ended with periods or, occasionally, exclamation points.)

> DIRECT QUESTION: Do you want a chocolate chip cookie?
> Do you know what he wants?

INDIRECT
QUESTION: I don't know whether he wants a chocolate chip cookie or not.
FRAGMENT: Chocolate chip cookie? What chocolate chip cookie?

Exclamation Points are used—occasionally—to signal the end of a sentence that expresses surprise or other strong emotions:

SENTENCE: I love carrot cake!
FRAGMENT: Carrot cake! Yummie!

Commas   (23b)

With Coordinating Conjunctions

Use a comma to join coordinate clauses when a coordinating conjunction precedes the second clause. The coordinating conjunctions are *and, but, so, yet, for, or,* and *nor*:

The low wage didn't depress her, *but* the high cost of living did.
Having her own apartment and her own car delighted her, *and*, in addition, her job was a challenge.

In Series

Use commas to separate the items in a series of words, phrases, or clauses of roughly equal importance:

They landed on the space station *Ariadne* despite an attack by an alien space ship, an epidemic of a fatal cosmic disease, an accidental time reversal, and an engine failure of monumental proportions.

Use commas to separate a series of coordinate adjectives but not a series of uncoordinate adjectives. The adjectives are coordinate if *and* can be inserted between the adjectives, and if the order of the modifiers can be reversed.

Eve felt a substantial, hard, definite lump in her old jacket pocket.
   could logically be:
Eve felt a substantial *and* hard *and* definite lump in her pocket.

Eve found a red sandstone rock in her old jacket pocket.
   could not be:
Eve found a red *and* sandstone rock. . . .

With Introductory Modifiers

Use a comma between an introductory modifier and the rest of the sentence:

Finally, the car started.
Although Joel knew her, Beth didn't know him.
Under the family room, there dwelt a family of mice.
Weaving in and out of the crowd, Martha finally caught up with him.

Do not confuse a gerund phrase that functions as the subject of the sentence with a participial phrase:

GERUND SUBJECT: Weaving the purple shawl was a pleasure for Martha.
PARTICIPIAL PHRASE: Having finished the purple shawl, she rested.

With Nonrestrictive Modifiers

Use commas to set off nonrestrictive modifiers, but do not use them with restrictive modifiers. A restrictive modifier is one that defines or limits the word it modifies, while a *nonrestrictive* modifier is one that adds information that is interesting but not necessary to understand the word in question. Nonrestrictive modifiers may be words, phrases, or clauses:

RESTRICTIVE: The woman whom he had loved for ten years came back.
NONRESTRICTIVE: The blue violets, *which are Aunt Ella's favorites*, bloomed.
RESTRICTIVE: The girl with the tousled curls came too.
NONRESTRICTIVE: The girl came too, *with hair tousled and hands dirty*.
RESTRICTIVE: The child dressed in a bear costume frightened the dog.
NONRESTRICTIVE: Colin, *dressed like a space man*, behaved himself.
RESTRICTIVE: The postlady is always late when she brings my check.
NONRESTRICTIVE: Miles loves the postlady, *whenever she comes*.
RESTRICTIVE: Our dog Don won a blue ribbon, but our Fifi did not.
NONRESTRICTIVE: Don, *our Labrador retriever*, is a very loving dog.

With Concluding Modifiers

Always separate concluding modifiers such as absolute and participial phrases from the main clause with commas:

Darnell is an engineer whose mechanical aptitude decreases with each step he takes closer to home, *his most famous repair resulting in routing hot water into the garden hose.*

With Transitional Expressions

Use commas to separate conjunctive adverbs and other transitions from the rest of the sentence, regardless of where in the sentence they appear:

Companies, however, are very specific.
Still, women account for only four to five percent of management.

In Direct Address

Use commas to set off the names of people being addressed:

Dr. Dearden, you know I tried hard!
We will go to Hawaii, Mr. Selleck, if you agree.

With Interjections

Use commas to set off interjections:

The Double Brass Band, as the name implies, is big and loud.

To Separate Quoted Matter

Commas that follow quotations should be placed inside the quotation marks. Commas separate nonquoted material from quoted matter:

"Dr. Nesbitt," they cried in unison, "let us hand our papers in next week!"

In Titles, Addresses, and Dates

When a person's name is followed by a degree or other title, it should be set off by commas:

Martin Luther King, Jr.
Elizabeth Barnes, Ph.D.

When a name with a title is part of a sentence, use a comma after the title as well:

The seminar speaker will be Jesse Billings, M.D., from Ohio.

Use a comma to set off the day of the month and the year:

I will arrive in Spain on May 15, 1985, at 10:45 A.M.

But omit the comma if only the month and year are used:

I will arrive in Spain May 1985.

Use commas to separate the elements in an address excepting the zip code:

My father has lived in Dedham, Massachusetts, all his life. His address is 123 Windsor Rd., Dedham, MA 02162

Semicolons (23c)

Use a semicolon to join two main clauses when there is no coordinating conjunction:

The Chicago Symphony Orchestra played a concert in Chicago on Tuesday; Wednesday night they played in Vienna.

Use a semicolon with a coordinating conjunction if the clauses are long or if there are many commas within the clauses:

The city soccer team lost on a Monday against Cleveland, 7–5; won on Friday against Moab, 16–0; lost again on the next Monday against Salt Lake City, 8–7; but won two games in a row this week, 6–5 and 7–3.

Colons (23d)

Use a colon to separate two independent clauses when the first one points ahead to the second and when the second one explains or amplifies the first:

> There are several courses that I need in order to graduate: a literature course will complete my humanities requirement; a biology course, my science requirement; and a Spanish class, my language.

Sometimes the second independent clause will be a quotation:

> The minister said in his sermon last Sunday: "Our lives are as successful as we let God make them."

While the part of the sentence before the colon must be a complete independent clause, the second part can be simply a list:

> These are the gifts Philip gave her: a gray cashmere sweater; a soft suede coat; and some seed pearl earrings.

Do not use a colon before a list if what precedes it is not a complete independent clause:

> Her pet peeves are people who honk at traffic lights, use swear words in conversation, and boast about their grandchildren.

Colons are also used in three conventional situations: a) before a subtitle; b) with the time of day; and c) with biblical citations:

> a) *The Vietnam War: The Aftermath*
> b) 2:00 A.M.
> c) Exodus 3:5–9

Dashes and Parentheses (23e)

Dashes and parentheses are sometimes used like commas to set off material that is related to the sentence but not necessary to its meaning:

> Mr. Bolding has a project planned to keep himself busy—and young— when he grows old.
> Mrs. Harris *(the Mrs. Harris who lives on Brown St.)* told me that they are planning to marry in June.

Problems in Sentence Punctuation   (23f)

Placing appropriate punctuation at the end of a sentence signals that it is complete. Your reader becomes confused if a period is placed after part of a sentence (fragment), a comma joins two sentences (comma splice), or a period is absent at the end of one sentence and the capital letter missing at the beginning of the next (fused sentence).

Sentence Fragments

When you use end punctuation, make certain that you are marking the end of a complete sentence. The most common kind of incomplete sentences, or *fragments,* results from punctuating phrases, clauses, or relative clauses as if they were full sentences:

> FRAGMENT: The flooding streets after it had poured all night.
> FRAGMENT: Which forced street crews out to clean the drains.
> SENTENCE: The streets flooded after it poured all night.
> SENTENCE: The heavy rain forced street crews out to clean the drains.
>   or:
> SENTENCE: The flooded streets, which forced work crews out to clean the drains, were the result of the heavy rain.

Comma Splices

When you place commas within a sentence, make certain that you are not splicing together two sentences which should be separated by a period or a semicolon, joined by a conjunction, or otherwise written as one sentence:

> My aunt took me to the library, she taught me to love fiction.
>   should be:
> My aunt took me to the library. She taught me to love fiction.
>   or:
> My aunt took me to the library where she taught me to love fiction.

Fused Sentences

Make certain that you place a period or other end punctuation after one complete sentence and a capital letter to start the one that follows:

> When the semester is over, he will be free for a while he will do those things he only dreams about now.

>   should be separated:

> When the semester is over, he will be free for a while. He will do those things he only dreams about now.

>   or joined by a semicolon and a conjunctive adverb:

When the semester is over, he will be free for a while; then, he will do those things he only dreams about now.

    or combined:

When the semester is over, he will be free to do those things he only dreams about now.

Exercise Objectives

Using periods, questions marks, and exclamation points; using commas, semi-colons, colons, dashes, and parentheses; recognizing and revising fragments, comma splices, and fused sentences.

13 PUNCTUATING SENTENCES _____

Name _____ *Date* _____

EXERCISE 1   Using Periods, Question Marks, and Exclamation Points

Punctuate the following letters with appropriate end punctuation. *Reminder: too many exclamation points will spoil a dramatic effect.*

Dear Joanna,

   This is just a note to thank you for your cards and calls I'm back at school, hobbling around on crutches but doing okay How do I feel Pretty good, actually The cast comes off next week Wish me luck

Thanks again,

Dear Belinda,

   I just got the brownies in the mail and ate about six of them They were delicious You've really helped me get through this broken-leg business with a minimum of the blues I wonder how you learned to be such a great cook I'm also wondering when I'll get to see you again How about the weekend of the twenty-fifth If that's not possible, will you please call me this week.

See you soon,

EXERCISE 2   Recognizing and Punctuating Direct and Indirect Questions

Place a question mark at the end of the direct questions below. Change all direct questions into indirect questions and write the revised sentences on the lines below. *Reminder: indirect questions end with a period.*

EXAMPLE
How would you like to go to see a movie tonight ?

Bob asked me if I wanted to go to a movie with him .

1. *(Joe to Marcia)* Did you ever sail in one of those thirty-foot sailboats __

_____

_____

2. *(Marcia to Joe)* Do you mean the kind that sleeps six and costs about twenty thousand dollars __

_____

_____

3. *(Barbara to Denise)* How would you feel if your best friend got the job you wanted __

_____

_____

4. *(Denise to Barbara)* How would you feel if it happened to you ___

_____

_____

5. *(Daughter to mother)* Do you regret getting married so young ___

_____

_____

Name _____ *Date* _____

EXERCISE 3 Using Commas Between Clauses

Combine each of the sentence groups to create one sentence composed of two independent clauses joined by a coordinating conjunction, and underline the comma.

EXAMPLE

I remember the house as gloomy and eerie.
I loved to play in the big hall, which was the darkest place of all.

I remember the house as gloomy and eerie, yet I loved to play in the big hall, which was the darkest place of all.

1. I was sent up to my room.
   I wasn't allowed to keep my presents.

   _____

   _____

2. Skipping breakfast didn't bother me.
   Skipping lunch and supper made me ravenous.

   _____

   _____

3. The man ahead of me ordered enough food for three people.
   It took a long time for his order to be filled.

   _____

   _____

4. Time and time again I find myself with the perfect noun, adjective, or verb on the tip of my tongue.
   I bite it back and spit out clichés instead.

   _____

   _____

5. The babysitter had to feed and burp the twins.
   He had to change them and do the laundry.

   _____

   _____

EXERCISE 4   Using Comma Between Items in a Series

The following sentences contain words, phrases, or clauses in series. Place commas between members of a series. *Reminder:* commas separate items in a series of three or more.

EXAMPLE
Searching his memory, finding an answer, and losing it again, the dazed man sought to determine his whereabouts.

1. He never seemed to tire of shaking hands signing autographs or dispensing advice.
2. Seated at the table with all her aunts uncles grandparents and dozens of cousins, Baby Sara commenced stuffing string beans in her ear.
3. She began boasting about her condo in Florida her boat her cruises and her fishing trips in the waters of the Florida Keys.
4. At one time a cook at another a painter and now a carpenter he loves to cook gourmet collect paintings and renovate old houses.
5. Big rigs pickups family cars and motorcycles pushed past the detour sign onto the highway and straight toward the collapsed bridge.

EXERCISE 5   Using Commas Between Coordinate Adjectives

The following sentences contain lists of adjectives. Place commas between coordinate adjectives and circle them. On the lines below, test the appropriateness of your revision by rewriting the sentence using *and* or by changing the order of the adjectives.

EXAMPLE
The wide, white, toothy grins of the barracuda arise from curiosity more than aggression.

The wide and white and toothy grins of the barracuda arise from curiosity more than aggression.

1. There we were six lost bawling children.

_____

_____

2. Suitable professional work clothes are expensive.

_____

_____

3. My mother was a tall strong wonderful woman.

_____

_____

4. Informal warm personal contacts must supplement formal programs.

_____

_____

5. Lee is an accommodating thoughtful generous man.

_____

_____

EXERCISE 6   Using Commas After Introductory Modifiers

The following sentences contain introductory materials that need separation from the main clauses by commas. Place a comma where needed, and circle it.

EXAMPLE
Having lost all her courage Betty turned and ran.

1. Near the car tires are piled in three stacks.
2. If I were a typical listener I would own dozens of tapes.
3. Finally I will discuss the implications of the research.
4. Because he tramples the flower beds Spot must be banished from the yard.
5. Running at full speed Donny charged the squirrel.

EXERCISE 7   Using Commas with Nonrestrictive Modifiers

The following sentences contain nonrestrictive clauses and phrases. Place commas in order to separate them from the rest of the sentence. Circle the commas.

EXAMPLE
The harbor at Cove Town which was battered by the hurricane last year is the place we moored in March.

1. Genevieve who is an underweight thin-faced woman watched tensely.
2. The teacher who is also our counselor spoke on the subject of racing.
3. I must have rattled my adversary whom I have now beaten three times.
4. One of the first things I learned about this college which my older brothers also attended is that there are dozens of clubs that hold open house. I go to all the open houses which of course serve munchies and eat enough for supper.
5. My old computer one of the first on the market continues to do its job.

EXERCISE 8 Using Commas with Concluding Modifiers

The following sentences end with words or phrases that should be separated from the main clause by a comma. Insert the comma at the appropriate place, and circle it

EXAMPLE
The children crawled around the floor⊙hunting for pennies.

1. The students underlined words and flipped pages bored with it all.
2. The gang grouped around Tony wolfing down pizzas drinking colas wiping their sticky hands on their levis.
3. He watched his son through the window his eyes following the haphazard movement the boy made with the rake.
4. She bombarded him with punches battering him all over with her tiny fists.
5. Susie looks like an expert her tiny fingers busily tapping the keys.

EXERCISE 9 Using Commas with Transitional Expressions

The following sentences contain transitional words and phrases. Insert commas in order to separate the phrases from the rest of the sentence. Circle the commas.

EXAMPLE
Beatrice⊙nevertheless⊙played beautifully.

1. I knew all along however that I would make it to the top.
2. The group is my favorite in the first place because of the lead singer.
3. The last question on the other hand is obscure.
4. The answer in fact is surprisingly clear.
5. Why then is it marked "incorrect"?

13 PUNCTUATING SENTENCES ⸺⸺⸺⸺⸺⸺

Name ⸺⸺⸺⸺⸺⸺⸺⸺⸺⸺⸺ *Date* ⸺⸺⸺⸺⸺

EXERCISE 10   Recognizing Direct Address and Interjections

The following sentences contain words of direct address or interjections. Place commas in order to separate these from the rest of the sentence. Circle the commas.

EXAMPLE
You may, of course, go home.

1. I want to compliment you Beatrice on how well you played.

2. James your socks don't match.

3. Yes they do match.

4. You must be I am sorry to say colorblind!

5. How important is the color of my socks Beatrice?

EXERCISE 11   Placing Commas in Order to Separate Quoted Matter

The following sentences contain quotations. Place commas needed to separate the quoted matter from the sentence. Circle the commas.

EXAMPLES
Rona moaned, "Take off my shoes," as she hobbled to the couch.

1. She began with a question "Who is your best friend?"

2. According to Joanne "The corpulent bureaucrats are eating our rations."

3. "No" said Peter's father "I will never agree to go."

4. "He was only twenty-three" the report said.

5. "You do not understand, Bill" she said "I am not coming back."

EXERCISE 12   Using Commas with Titles, Addresses, and Dates

In the following sentences, the commas are missing. Place them where they belong, and circle them.

EXAMPLE
The seminar will be held on March 11, 1985, at 7:00 P.M. in State Hall.
The speaker will be Joanna Norris, M.D., from Troy.

1. Mrs. Phillips is staying at the Carlton Hotel between May 15 1985 and January 2 1986.

2. Claire Tree Ph.D. has an office in the Fisher Towers at 3011 Grand Street Detroit Michigan 48202.

3. The expiration date of the contest is May 1986. Send in your poems and stories on or before April 30 1986 to Contest at 154 Wayne Avenue Moab Utah 84532.

4. Holley Martin Sr. came from Florida for the birthday party.

5. Dear Holley   103 West Ave. Dearborn MI 48226

                                                      January 12 1986

Thank you for the birthday gift.

                                                          Yours truly

                                                          Bill Jr.

Name _____ *Date* _____

EXERCISE 13   Using Semicolons Between Independent Clauses

Separate the following independent clauses with a semicolon instead of a comma. Mark the semicolon above the place that it belongs, and circle it.

EXAMPLE

Damon is a psychologist⨟ his wife, Mary, is an orthopedist.

1. There was little doubt who would win the election, James had such a persuasive speaking style that he was a shoo-in.

2. The chair of the Chemistry Department suggested that I write a letter of complaint about my instructor, other than that, she had no advice to give me.

3. My boss wasn't impressed by my sob story, she had heard this song before.

4. For starters, I'd say we need two hundred dollars, after we get back from Fort Lauderdale, we'll work out who owes what.

5. He's not heavy, he's my brother.

EXERCISE 14   Using Semicolons and Commas with Conjunctive Adverbs

Mark the semicolon above the place that it belongs, and circle it. Place commas where needed to separate conjunctive adverbs from the clauses they introduce, and circle the commas.

EXAMPLE

We had stocked up on chips and soft drinks ⓢ however ⓒ we had forgotten the nutritious things like meat, vegetables, and milk.

1. The problem with natural gas deregulation is that wellhead prices might rise dramatically however the most important issue is the ultimate distribution of income between producers and consumers.

2. Natalie dreaded making the several hundred pastries she had promised for her sister's wedding nevertheless she good-naturedly set to work.

3. Many newly developed diagnostic techniques are less invasive to the patient than X rays however because of the sophisticated technology involved, costs are prohibitively expensive.

4. The workers did a poor job laying the subflooring consequently the small nails began working their way up through the tiles.

5. There is a wealth of talent among modern jazz composers and musicians indeed some people feel that jazz will become tomorrow's classical music.

Name _____ *Date* _____

EXERCISE 15 Using Colons

In the following, place colons where they are needed. Mark the colon in the place that it belongs, and circle it. If you think that semicolons are needed in the sentence, include them.

EXAMPLE

We looked at every kind of living quarters⊙studio apartments, a mini mansion, and a charming flat in an old neighborhood.

1. Medical diagnosticians can now perform noninvasive tests for the following anatomical abnormalities in the brain and chest, Alzheimer's disease, brain tumors, and diseases of the kidney and liver.

2. Technical writing students will learn the following to write a long formal report, to write as a member of a team, and to complement their written presentations with oral reports.

3. One critic claims that the issues in American novels are various "the issues central to the American novel have been and still are America as the new Garden of Eden, the American as the new Adam, and the moral issues implicit in the confrontation of the civilized world with the primitive."

4. By 8 00 A.M. in the morning, the crime had been solved at 3 00 A.M. the gun had been found, at 4 00 A.M. the culprit had been identified, by 7 00 A.M. he had been caught, and at 8 00 A.M. he confessed.

5. The imagery central to an understanding of *Finders Keepers The Lost Children* can be found in passages that describe the parents' response to losing the children and the kidnappers' emotions while stealing them.

EXERCISE 16   Using Dashes and Parentheses

Include parentheses or dashes to enclose parenthetical material. *Reminder:* dashes dramatize parenthetical material and parentheses reduce its importance. In addition, sometimes dashes precede a series. Mark the dashes above the place that they belong.

EXAMPLE

I removed the pin from the bomb very slowly ⎯ better safe than sorry ⎯ and successfully defused it.

1. Rosalie loved me at least I thought she loved me for one whole year.

2. The book holds the students' attention and teaches meaningful facts and ideas e.g., pages 44–49.

3. The meaning desired by readers arises out of some sort of conflict a clash of actions, ideas, or desires.

4. Something had come into life into our lives that we had never known before.

5. Producing an almost automatic response in some readers are certain situations and objects babies, mothers, grandmothers, young love, and patriotism.

Name _____ Date _____

EXERCISE 17   Recognizing and Revising Sentence Fragments

In the word groups below, underline the sentence fragments. Revise the groups so that the fragment is combined logically with the sentence to make one complete sentence.

EXAMPLE

She smiled again. <u>That smile that always melted John's heart.</u>

She smiled again with that smile that always melted John's heart.

1. It had been a long, hard day. Which had had its high points, as well as its lows.

   _____

   _____

2. Imaginative techniques are making possible the study of biochemistry *in vivo.* Although the high cost of such techniques may keep them from widespread distribution.

   _____

   _____

   _____

3. Boris looking serious. I hardly knew what to expect from him.

   _____

   _____

4. To feel sad on such a gray, rainy Sunday, which should have been a beautiful day for the picnic. I guess it is normal to feel this way.

   _____

   _____

5. Mr. Alloway gave his daughter a new convertible. Which she impressed her friends no end.

   _____

   _____

6. He took her to the amusement park. Hoping to satisfy her demand for excitement where all the rides are.

_____

_____

7. Reupholstering the chair which Miranda kept putting off. It was a tedious job.

_____

_____

8. He lost his job. Not because of anything he did, but because the radio station changed hands.

_____

_____

9. If Mark brings his car to his cousin for repair. Then, he will get a good deal.

_____

_____

10. Jumping up and down and gesturing wildly as he attempted to get her attention. She didn't see him. Now flying to London without her glasses, which she will need in the museums.

_____

_____

_____

Name _____ *Date* _____

EXERCISE 18   Recognizing and Revising Comma Splices

Correct the following comma splices using the technique indicated. Mark the corrections above the place in which they belong.

Technique: Separate two sentences (independent clauses) with a period, and begin the second clause with a capital letter.

EXAMPLE

Welcome to St. Valentine's Day 1985, the modern world has gained satellite communication and lost the love letter.

1. "Where is my hockey stick?" he asked himself, "It is in the hall closet," was his answer.
2. In boxing, two men are thrown together within the confines of the ring, with a minimum of equipment they hit each other until one is unable to continue.
3. Just suppose you are a thirty-eight-year-old housewife, a mother of two sons, how do you feel as a freshman in college?

Technique: Join the two sentences (independent clauses) with a conjunction.

4. Her funds are shrinking, she looks desperately for work.
5. The degree of speed and agility possessed by good hockey players separates them from mediocre ones, physical strength added to these other qualities make a professional.
6. I love outside work, I work behind a bank teller's window.

Technique: Use a semicolon with a conjunctive adverb.

7. The legend of the First Division began as a simple maneuver, however, it soon became a large-scale attack.
8. Our men made a courageous charge across the beachhead, consequently, thirty of them lost their lives.
9. Tennis is fun to play and also encourages friendships, moreover, it develops physical fitness and stamina.

Technique: Embed one clause in the other.

10. Christmas is a time for giving and receiving gifts, it is a time for sharing a feeling of good will.

_____

_____

11. Before 1970 television could be watched by everyone, it was not too violent for children.

_____

_____

12. It is important to get good grades and to satisfy the credit requirements of the College of Business, I will, as a result, receive a bachelor's degree.

_____

_____

Technique: Use any of the above.
13. Every day people encounter "shape-up" techniques, one day it is yoga, the next it is running.

_____

_____

14. My mother has had a strong influence on me, she has always been there, she has given me advice.

_____

_____

15. Many people say violence is part of the game these days, therefore, we must expect it wherever we go.

_____

_____

Name _____ *Date* _____

EXERCISE 19   Recognizing and Revising Fused Sentences

The following independent clauses are fused into one sentence. Revise them by placing a period at the end of the first and a capital at the beginning of the second clause, by using coordination, a semicolon and a conjunctive adverb, or by combining the two clauses. Write the revised sentence on the line below.

EXAMPLE
I will give the reader some facts about martial arts I will discuss why they are useful and how to attain proficiency.

I will tell the reader why martial arts are useful and how to attain proficiency in them.

1. One of the ways to capture happy occasions is to learn how to take pictures many different kinds of cameras are available to you.

_____

_____

2. Each year the O'Reillys come from miles away to get together for one day to strengthen family ties therefore, I have been to several family reunions.

_____

_____

_____

3. David should be walking in a few months in fact by June he will be a toddler.

_____

_____

4. The shutter-speed dial lets one decide how long the film should be exposed the slower the shutter speed the longer the film is exposed.

_____

_____

5. Preindustrial America had a phenomenon known as "courtship" interested parties became familiar with each other through this ritual.

_____

_____

EXERCISE 20   Examining the Punctuation in Your Own Writing

Write a letter to a classmate describing your activities on the day before a paper is due or an exam is scheduled. In addition to the description, include an explanation of your feelings about these activities in view of your academic responsibilities. Exchange your letter with your classmate and discuss with him or her the significance of what you both have written. Make certain that your punctuation guides your reader clearly through the letter.

14

PUNCTUATION OF WORDS

Hyphens (24a)

Hyphens are used to join words.
  Hyphens join two words that are so closely related they act as one word:

> They played a *double-header*.

Hyphens join two words that act as a single modifier:

> Our *good-neighbor* policy won recognition.

A hyphen joins compound numbers from twenty-one to ninety-nine:

> The cost is *forty-five* dollars a day.

If two or more hyphenated words belong to the same base, both should be hyphenated:

> The amount is either *forty-* or *sixty-one* dollars.

Use a hyphen between a prefix and its word if the meaning is not clear without the hyphen:

> She will *recover* the stolen money.
> Barbara wants to *re-cover* the porch furniture.

Hyphens often follow the prefixes *anti-*, *pro-*, *self-*, and *ex-*. They precede the suffix *-elect:*

> The *ex-president* attended the celebration.
> The *president-elect* played in the golf tournament.

Apostrophes (24b)

Apostrophes mark possession and, in certain instances, plurals. They also help form contractions.

An apostrophe plus an *s* indicates possession: *'s* forms singular and *s'* forms plural possession:

> The sto*re's* reputation was damaged.
> The sto*res'* reputations were damaged.

An apostrophe is sometimes used with an *s* to form the plural of numbers and abbreviations:

> Charles saw two UFO*'s* last night.
> Susan confuses her *v's* with *b's*.

Apostrophes help shorten certain forms in casual and informal writing to make contractions:

> He could*n't* face her.

Underlining (Italics) (24c)

Underlining in handwritten and typed materials signals that the words marked in this way will appear in italics in the printed essay. Published works, works of art, television programs, record albums, names of vehicles, many foreign words, and letters and numbers under discussion are underlined as a direction to italicize. (Some writers will also underline words that they want to stress.)

> First I finished Walker's <u>The Color Purple,</u> and then I listened to Mozart's <u>Don Giovanni</u>.
> That is <u>not</u> a course of action I recommend.

Quotation Marks (24d)

Quotation marks set off sections of writing, speech, or poetry copied from other sources. In addition, they mark the titles or chapters within a collection or a book. Sometimes they call attention to a word that is used in a sense different from ordinary usage.

Use quotation marks to enclose words spoken by characters in a narration or a dialogue. In a dialogue, each person's speech is indented as if it were a separate paragraph, and closely related phrases such as "he said" are included in the paragraph with the speech:

> Lynn saw David on the mall. He was by himself and loaded with books.
> She called to him, "Did you go to the game?"
> "No," he shouted back, "I had to work overtime checking inventory, and I had a paper to write. Besides, I didn't want to go alone."

Wherever someone else's words are recorded, place quotation marks around them:

One researcher comments, "The countries with higher fat consumption continue to have high cancer rates."

Use quotation marks around the titles of chapters, essays, short stories, songs, poems, newspaper articles, and magazine or journal articles:

Have you read "The Processing of RNA" in this month's *Scientific American?*

Use quotation marks around words used in a special sense.

Our program's "quality" teaching is producing poor readers.

Follow these rules while punctuating with quotation marks:

Periods and commas always go inside quotation marks:

Jamie reported first, "The sky is black," and then changed her mind and said, "The sky is greenish black, foreboding."

Colons and semicolons always go outside quotation marks:

Louis said aggressively, "Of course I can drive"; however, it turned out that he couldn't.

Normally, a comma is used after words introducing the quotation. Other marks of punctuation go inside or outside quotation marks depending on whether they are part of the quoted material:

I asked Jill, "Can you drive?"
Did Jill say, "Yes, I can drive"?

Use single quotation marks to set off a quotation within a quotation:

The reporter said, "If I understand your answer correctly, you said, 'absolutely never.' "

Lengthy quotations should be presented in block form, indented, and without quotation marks. Since the double quotation marks are absent, the single quotations within these long quotations become double quotation marks.

Ellipses and Brackets   (24e)

Even though quotations should report word for word what the source has said, dropping an irrelevant word or phrase and adding a word may clarify the meaning of the quotation in the context of the essay in which it is used.

If a word or phrase is deleted, an ellipsis should mark the spot from which it has been removed. If the ellipsis occurs at the end of the sentence, mark the period and then the ellipsis (a total of four spaced points).

The following text was used as the source for the quotation below it:

> "The baseball coach says that he has coached here a long time—ever since he moved up from the south—but he has never seen players as brilliant as Erin and Eric. 'They are our newest recruits,' he says, 'but when I tell them to play ball, they are twin geniuses in hitting and fielding.' "

The following quotation employs block form, uses ellipses, and changes single quotation marks to double:

> The baseball coach says that he has coached here a long time . . . but he has never seen players as brilliant as Eric and Erin. "They are our newest recruits," he says, "but when I tell them to play ball, they are twin geniuses. . . ."

A bracket is used to enclose an editorial comment or a word inserted to clarify the quotation:

> "Stavros pretends to buy the story that she [Laura] has amnesia."
> "Lily's personality changes, bringing to the forefront her evil self. Lorna [the name of the evil self] abuses the children and batters Curtis."

Capitalization   (24f)

Capital letters begin sentences, indicate titles of books, plays, and other artistic productions, and are the first letter in proper nouns.

1. *You should capitalize:*
   The first word of a sentence.
   The first letter of the first and last words of a title, as well as other words except articles (a, an, the), conjunctions, and prepositions of four letters or less.
   The first letter within a quotation unless it is the continuation of a sentence.
   The first letter of each line of traditional poetry.
   The first word of a sentence that follows a colon if the sentence is strong or important.
   The interjection *O* and the pronoun *I*, but not *oh*.

> The most memorable character in *The Lord of the Flies* is Simon.
> The reaction was dramatic: Three people ran to the back of the room, and two ran out the door; *I* fainted. "Oh, oh!" said the snake handler. "They must have gotten out."

2. *You should capitalize:*
   Names of real or fictional people, personifications of objects, or concepts, and titles of people.

William Shakespeare   Shakespearean actor
Donald Duck   Copernican cosmos
Old Man River   Aurora (dawn)   Wagnerian opera
The Reverend Rudolph Smith
Joanne Beaupre, Dean of the College of Liberal Arts
Governor Clinton and Uncle Earl

Full titles and shorter titles of address should be capitalized, but when a title word is used as a general class rather than as a term of address, it is not capitalized.

Dr. Beaupre was appointed *dean.*
We heard a *governor* and a *congressman* speak.
Aunt Mary remembers me, but my *uncle* doesn't.
I often see the *doctor* but not much of Grandfather Carlton.

3. *You should capitalize:*
   Names of languages, ethnic groups, regions, and places, and adjectives derived from them.

   English, English language
   Arab, Arabic numbers
   Black Americans, Black history
   Canada, Canadian side of the river
   Ontario   Toronto   Oulette Avenue   Bloomfield Hills
   Pacific Ocean   Lake Superior   Au Sable River
   Capricorn   Hunter's Canyon   Escort (car)
   Sea Spray (ship)   *Challenger II* (space shuttle)

4. *You should capitalize:*
   Names of historical periods, events, and documents; political groups and bodies, lodges and civic organizations; names of companies and corporations; teams in sports and cultural institutions.

   the Middle Ages   the Treaty of Ghent
   Battle of Bull Run   World War I
   Declaration of Independence   British Parliament
   the Democratic Party   the Tiger, Bear, or Piston teams
   the University of Michigan

When words like *battle, treaty,* and *parliament* are used to refer to a general class, they are *not* capitalized.

The battle was over and the treaty was signed.

5. *You should capitalize:*
   Religions, religious groups, the supreme being, and other religious terms and adjectives derived from them.

God   the Lord   the Bible   Christianity   Baptist
Buddha   Allah   Islam   Islamic   Koran

Days, months, holidays, and holy days (seasons are *not* capitalized).

March   Monday   Christmas
Yom Kippur   Independence Day

Abbreviations   (24g)

A few abbreviations are always acceptable in writing; some are never acceptable.

1. *You should abbreviate:*
   In front of a name: Mr., Ms., Mrs., Dr., and St. (saint), Dr. Kapordelis; St. Thomas.
   If followed by a given and surname: Hon., Gen., Gov., Sgt., and Rev., Sgt. Harlow Billings; Rev. Trevor Jones; Gov. Jim Brickton
2. *You should not abbreviate:*
   Both before *and* after a name; use either Dr. Mary Bilitis *or* Mary Bilitis, M.D.
   Names of streets, states, countries (except U.S.A. and U.S.S.R.), months, days, measures, and the words *page, chapter, volume,* and *line,* except in bibliography and documentation.
   Words such as *company (co.), corporation (corp),* and *and (&)* unless the official title of the company is written that way.
3. *You should abbreviate:*
   Words with numerals:

   2:30 P.M. or A.M.   no. 32
   239 B.C. or BC   A.D. 1099 or AD 1099

4. *You should not* use periods in acronyms made from abbreviating names or organizations or other groups of words:
   AMA (American Medical Association)
   UN (United Nations)
   NOW (National Organization of Women)
   GNP (gross national product)
5. *You may use certain Latin abbreviations:*

   ca. (approximately); *etc.* (and so forth); *cf.* (compare); *i.e.* (that is); *e.g.* (for example); *et al.* (and others); *viz.* (namely)

Numbers   (24h)

Spell out numbers that are under one hundred and that take one or two words to write.

Six or sixty-three,
    but
663 or 6,663

Use numbers for the time, the date, time periods, decimals, and percentages; for acts, scenes and lines in a play.

On January 15, 1892, at 2:00 A.M. only 20 percent of the people in Pointe Village could sleep. The remainder were kept awake because the Pointe Players were practicing with live ammunition the battle scene from Act III, Scene iii, of their new play.

Exercise Objectives

Understanding how to use hyphens, apostrophes, quotation marks, italics, ellipses, and brackets; capitals, abbreviations, and numbers.

14 PUNCTUATION OF WORDS ⎯⎯⎯⎯⎯⎯⎯

Name ⎯⎯⎯⎯⎯⎯⎯⎯⎯⎯⎯⎯⎯⎯⎯ *Date* ⎯⎯⎯⎯⎯⎯

EXERCISE 1   Using Hyphens to Join Compound Words

Look in the dictionary for the words underlined below to determine whether they are compound words needing a hyphen. Rewrite the words in their revised form on the blank to the right.

EXAMPLE

The flag was at <u>half mast</u>. *half-mast* ⎯⎯⎯⎯⎯⎯⎯⎯

1. The police discovered his <u>hide out</u>. ⎯⎯⎯⎯⎯⎯⎯⎯

2. We found an old <u>jail house</u>. ⎯⎯⎯⎯⎯⎯⎯⎯

3. I entrust you with her <u>well being</u>. ⎯⎯⎯⎯⎯⎯⎯⎯

4. Ozaw is a <u>delegate at large</u>. ⎯⎯⎯⎯⎯⎯⎯⎯

5. The <u>love making</u> of the bees amazes me. ⎯⎯⎯⎯⎯⎯⎯⎯

EXERCISE 2   Using Hyphens to Join Words Used as Single Modifiers

Nouns in the following sentences have more than one adjective. Join with a hyphen those that can function as single-word modifiers. Mark the hyphen above the place that it belongs.

EXAMPLE
This hand‾me‾down coat has lasted a long time.

1. The sleep inducing motion finally stopped.

2. My father gave me the go ahead signal.

3. The air raid shelter was hidden under the stairs.

4. Bessie, an all around athlete, won the medal.

5. The ill managed event angered Phyllis.

6. His well bred manner never left him.

7. I went to an eye ear nose throat specialist.

8. Mark was assigned the follow up story.

9. Jessica doesn't like ready made clothes.

10. I live at the end of a dead end street.

EXERCISE 3 Using Hyphens with Numbers and with Two or More Hyphenated Words That Belong to a Common Base

Write out the sentences below, both spelling out numbers where appropriate and putting hyphens where needed.

EXAMPLE
He read in 20 to 40 minute segments.

He read in twenty- to forty-minute segments.

1. I have saved 365 Superman comic books, which span a 13 or 14 year period.

_____

2. 33 is a magic age.

_____

3. I dislike 6 and 10 week semesters.

_____

4. She appeared to be pro and anti war at the same time.

_____

5. The bride was nervous about meeting her new mother and father in law.

_____

EXERCISE 4 Using Hyphens at Syllable Breaks

Look for the following words in the dictionary and hyphenate them where syllable breaks occur. *Reminder:* some words cannot be hyphenated.

EXAMPLE
informative *in-form-a-tive*

1. limousine _____
2. like _____
3. picture _____
4. strength _____
5. complement _____

6. protect _____
7. handy _____
8. strategy _____
9. really _____
10. protection _____

Name ————————————————————— *Date* —————————

EXERCISE 5   Using *'s* or *s'*

Revise the following sentences so as to use *'s* or *s'*. Write the revised sentences on the lines below. *Reminder:* certain nouns have a different spelling in the plural (*women, children, geese,* etc.) and take *'s*. For many more exercises on the possessive see chapter 6, exercises 5–11.

EXAMPLE
The boyfriend of Jane came to the door.

Jane's boyfriend came to the door.

1. The sweater of Nora was brightly beaded.

—————————————————————————————————

2. The coats of the men were covered with braid.

—————————————————————————————————

3. The blouses of the children were purple silk.

—————————————————————————————————

4. The secretary planned the schedule of the doctor carefully.

—————————————————————————————————

5. The tour guide planned the schedules of the travelers carefully.

—————————————————————————————————

6. The color of the moss is gray.

—————————————————————————————————

7. The ears of the rabbits pointed upward.

—————————————————————————————————

8. The quilts of the women were colorful.

—————————————————————————————————

9. The road maps of the three counties were identical.

—————————————————————————————————

10. The tails of the mice were skinny.

—————————————————————————————————

EXERCISE 6   Using Apostrophes for Contractions

Rewrite the following sentences to include contractions. *Reminder:* the apostrophe usually indicates that a letter is omitted.

EXAMPLE

I cannot.   _I can't._

1. You do not. _____

2. She does not. _____

3. We must not! _____

4. Who could not? _____

5. It is not! _____

6. He will not. _____

7. I am not! _____

8. You have not. _____

9. She has not. _____

10. They are. _____

EXERCISE 7   Using Underlining for Italics

In the following sentences, certain words, phrases, and numbers should be italicized. Underline these parts of the sentences.

EXAMPLE

I saw for the first time an <u>Ampullaria glauca</u> in her shell collection.

1. Some of the most famous of the general's big words are epistemological-wise and definitizing.

2. Jameson, Kenneth. Algebra and Ordinary People. The Journal of High School Mathematics. 44, 635–650.

3. Bill and I spent a quiet week aboard the Princess, reading Dorothy Sayers' Gaudy Night.

4. Voyager 2 is gathering information about our solar system.

5. We read The New York Times and watched 60 Minutes on television.

Name _____ *Date* _____

EXERCISE 8 Punctuating Narrative and Dialogue

The following narrative, which includes dialogue, needs to be indented and punctuated. Revise the paragraph and write the revision on the lines below.

Little Red Riding Hood cheerfully approached her grandmother's bed. She was somewhat surprised at her grandmother's appearance. She said grandmother what big eyes you have. The better to see you with my dear the grandmother said. Grandmother, what big ears you have said the little girl. The better to hear you with said the grandmother. Finally Little Red Riding Hood said grandmother why do you have such big teeth. The grandmother said loudly the better to eat you with my dear. Help! said the little girl.

_____

_____

_____

_____

_____

_____

_____

_____

_____

EXERCISE 9   Using Quotation Marks with Other Punctuation

In the following items, place and circle quotation marks and other punctuation where needed.

EXAMPLE

He said fervently, "I won't forget your birthday," but the next year he did forget.

1. Are you going home he queried.

   I am going she responded but not home

2. Which person said are you going home

3. Brian Brill describes his visit to his eighty-five year old Grandmother who had begun repeating things: Grandmother and I would always have the

same conversation. Hello, Hello She would say I read your book, read your book. Ive read it twice she would continue Twice. Wonderful, wonderful I would say.

4. Did you watch Three's Company on television last night he asked. Watch television! I am reading Milton's Lycidas I answered

5. When we entered the Louvre, she said we headed straight for the Mona Lisa however we never noticed the Winged Victory.

6. My aunt tells this story about my uncle Peter's favorite hymn is Onward Christian Soldiers however he missed the song entirely because of his preoccupation with the book he had hidden in the hymnal which contained the stories of Sinbad the Sailor and Vernon Bold Cowboy Hero.

7. Have you had a chance to read What is Matter by Bertrand Russell from your textbook Writing About Science

8. I settled down to read a long article in the Detroit Free Press entitled American Arab Women.

9. He summed up the plot in these words the good people turned their backs on the problem and the bad people went outside and gave their hungry friends a helping hand.

10. Donaldson, George. Who is Billy Sims Sportsmen's Magazine Apr. 1985, pp 16–23.

Name ——————————————————— *Date* ——————————

EXERCISE 10   Using Brackets and Ellipses in a Quotation

The source below has been used in 1 and 2 to construct quotations. Compare these quotations to the source, and supply quotation marks where needed. Where parts of the quotation have been dropped, place the necessary ellipsis marks above the line; where information has been added inside the quotation, insert brackets.

The italicized phrases are the parts of the paragraph that introduce the quotation or complete the paragraph.

Source: The idea was controversial because it had seldom, if ever, been tried before. Animal experts scoffed when they heard it. Once tamed, they said, no lion would ever be able to hunt, mate and rear cubs. But the Adamsons proved the experts wrong. Not only did Elsa succeed in fending for herself; she also kept in touch with her human "parents" long after she had left home. (Houston 101)

Reference: Houston, Dick, "An Old African Hand Fights to Keep His Lions Wild and Free." *Smithsonian* July 1983: 98–106.

BLOCK QUOTATION

1. *George Adamson, well known because of the movie "Born Free," made about him and a lioness, first suggested the possibility of returning a tame animal to the wilderness. Dick Houston in a biographical article on Adamson says that when this idea was introduced it was thought impossible, but Adamson proved otherwise:*

The idea was controversial because it had seldom, if ever, been tried before. Animal experts scoffed when they heard about it. Once tame, they said, no lion would ever be able to hunt, mate and rear cubs. Not only did Elsa the lioness succeed in fending for herself; she also kept in touch long after she had left home. (101)

Now, many animals besides Elsa have been introduced successfully to the wilds.

INTEGRATED QUOTATION

2. *When the possibility of returning a tame animal to the wilderness was suggested, the experts said it was impossible. No doubt,* The idea was controversial because it had seldom, if ever, been tried before. But the Adamsons proved the experts wrong. Not only did Elsa succeed in fending for herself when they returned her to the wilderness; she also kept in touch with her human parents (Houston 101).

EXERCISE 11   Punctuating a Quotation

Imagine that you want to quote parts of the source below. Because of the way your essay (on the subject of marathons) is composed, you have decided that you don't need details from this quotation such as numbers, ages, and historical designations. Write on the lines below a version of a quotation which meets the requirements of your essay and for which you provide punctuation as needed.

Source: Many people of all ages, a few in their sixties and seventies, several between thirty and forty, and many in their twenties—even one with a baby on her back, crossed the finish line. This was the largest group that had ever finished the event in all of its fifteen years.

_____

_____

_____

_____

_____

14 PUNCTUATION OF WORDS

Name _____ Date _____

EXERCISE 12   Using Capitals

The following sentences need to be edited for correct use of capitals. Wherever a capital is needed, underline the letter to be capitalized three times (≡).

EXAMPLE
the book i read last saturday was *huckleberry finn*.

1. the shakespearean actor explained the newtonian physics in both english and french.

2. first, joe flew over the grand canyon and then landed near the colorado river. travelling the river by raft, he saw lizards and an american skink of the genus *eumeces* and at night he saw orion.

3. we flew to san francisco on a republic airline 767 where we transferred to the *orient star* for a water voyage to the far east.

4. she gave her children names from the bible hoping that god would look kindly on them.

5. in eastern michigan around the city of detroit, there is an ethnic mix of poles, germans, italians, mexicans, arabs, and american blacks.

6. the battle of the bulge took place in world war II.

7. If you visit boston you can see the hancock building, faneuil hall, and the home of the boston symphony orchestra.

8. Felicia Hemans in the poem "the landing of the pilgrim fathers" describes the first landing of these brave men and women at plymouth rock

> the breaking waves dashed high
>
> on a stern and rock-bound coast,
>
> and the woods against a stormy sky,
>
> their giant branches tost. . . .

9. We met the dean at the christmas party. All I could think of to say was "o!" Sheila, however, having met her before said, "dean moore, I think we met at professor riswell's last september."

10. I saw a cartoon in which the pink panther leaped over castle rock and was then run over by a general motors corporation product.

EXERCISE 13   Using Abbreviations and Numbers

In the following sentences, there are several inaccuracies in the use of abbreviations and numbers. Circle the error and write the sentence using the correct form on the lines below.

EXAMPLE

An organization funding the G̶O̶P̶is located on the ave̶near
Gov̶Raine's headquarters.

An organization funding the GOP is located on the
avenue near Governor Raine's headquarters.

1. Dr. George Jungles M.D. complained to Prof. Snowden that he couldn't find the Feb. report.

_____

_____

2. I was no. six-hundred and thirty-five on the list in Jan. and no. 554 in Apr. This month I am number two-hundred.

_____

_____

3. Ford Motor Co. and General Motors Corp. are selling twenty.5 percent more cars in nineteen-hundred and eighty-five.

_____

_____

4. Jean gained 20 lbs and grew 1 ft. in the last year.

_____

_____

5. Dear Doctor George Beeman,
    On Sept. 3 1986 at 2 00 PM I have an app't with you. It is 6 yrs. since I have seen a Dr., and I am concerned over the cost in $ of this visit. . . .

_____

_____

REVIEWING THE
WRITING PROCESS

Name ————————————————— *Date* —————————

FINAL EXERCISE: **Writing About Your Own Writing Process**

Return to chapter 1 to review the steps in the writing process. Examine your own writing process as you experienced it while writing the paragraphs and essays assigned in this book. Compose an essay in which you describe your own particular process. Do not hesitate to describe activities that are unique to you. A part of the paper may deal with the effort you spent in constructing paragraphs and sentences, and in revising word choice, punctuation, and spelling.

INDEX

Boldface page numbers indicate exercises.

abbreviations, 290, **302**
-able, -ible, 239, **247**
absolute phrases, 80, **83**, 172
  commas with, 261
  in cumulative sentences, 172
active voice, 100, **120**, 173-174, **191,**
  196, 207-208
adjectives, 51, 56, **73-74**, 161-163, **165-**
  170
  absolute, 163, **168-170**
  adverbs confused with, 161, **165**, 56,
    75-76
  comparative forms of, 162-163, **167-**
    168
  coordinate, commas between, 260
  introductory modifiers as, 260
  after linking verbs, 161, **165**
  modified by adverbs, 161
  negative, 163
  participial, 56, **74**
  sentences expanded with, 173, **183-**
    186
  superlative forms of, 162
  used as adverbs, 161
adverbs, 51, 56, 161-163, **165-170**
  adjectives confused with, 56, **75-76,**
    161, **165**
  comparative forms of, 162-163, **167-**
    168
  conjunctive, 57
  placement of, 195-196
  sentences expanded with, 82, 173,
    183-186
  superlative forms of, 162-163, **167-**
    168
agreement, 145-148, **149-160**
  with collective nouns, 147, **155**
  with compound subjects, 146, **153**
  with foreign plurals, 147-148
  general rules of, 145-148
  with indefinite pronouns, 148, **156**
  with linking verbs, 148-149, **159**

prepositional phrases and, 148, **157**
  of pronoun and antecedent, 145-146,
    151-152, 159
  relative clauses and, 148, **157-158**
  of subject and verb, 145-146, **149-50,**
    159
-ally, -ly, 239, **248**
analogy,
  in developing a thesis, 5, 7
  ordering of, 8
antecedents, **44-46**
  agreement of pronouns and, 145-146,
    151-152
  unclear, **44**
apostrophes, 286, **295-296**
  in contractions, 286
  for plurals, 286
  for possession, 286
appositives, 52, **64**
arranging, 8-10, **19-30**
audience, 4-5, **13-14**
auxiliary verbs, 96, **109, 111**
  in compound verb forms, 96-97
  modal, 96
  in passive voice, 100

be,
  as auxiliary verb, 96
  inflection of, 93-94
  in subjunctive mood, 95
beginnings, 9, **27-29**
books,
  punctuating titles of, 263, 287-288
brackets, 287-288, **299-300**
  for insertions, 288

capitalization, 259, 288-290, **301**
  of first word in sentence, 288
  in poetry, 288
  of titles, 288